From Osborne House
to Wheatfen Broad

Memoirs of Phyllis Ellis,
collected and edited by
Pete Kelley

published by
Wheatfen Books

First published by Wheatfen Books November 2011

© 2011 Wheatfen Books, Norwich UK

http://www.wheatfen.com

Designed by Marion Catlin and Suzie Hanna

Typeset in Perpetua

Printed by BD&H Ltd, Norwich UK

ISBN 978-0-9571094-0-7

Cover photograph: Phyllis Ellis at Wheatfen in 1953

Illustrations by Ted Ellis from his collection

CONTENTS

With grateful thanks to the family, neighbours and friends of Phyllis Ellis

Phyllis in her 80s

INTRODUCTION

During the 1990s Pete Kelley, who wrote '*The People's Naturalist*', a biography of Ted Ellis, under the pseudonym Eugene Stone, recorded weekly conversations with our mother Phyllis, then in her eighties, in which she reminisced about her life. These took place walking around the woods and marshes or sitting by the fire in her home.

Phyllis was the wife of Ted Ellis, the celebrated Norfolk naturalist, writer and broadcaster. After his death in 1986 she was instrumental in setting up the Ted Ellis Nature Reserve at Wheatfen Broad on the River Yare near Norwich and became a well-known figure as a speaker in her own right. Aged 83 in 1996 she received an MBE for Services to Nature Conservation, after which she took up abseiling for charity, continuing with this activity until she was 88 years old.

Her great-grandfather was head gamekeeper to Queen Victoria at Osborne House on the Isle of Wight. The Queen herself chose the site of his grave and attended his funeral. As children we had, in our dressing-up box, a piece of the veil which she had worn after Albert's death.

At Sudbourne Hall in Suffolk she was a childhood playmate of Kenneth Clark (Lord Clark of '*Civilisation*' fame) and she paints a vivid picture of life there during the early part of the 20th century.

Phyllis was familiar to readers of the Eastern Daily Press and Country Living amongst other publications and she has already appeared in several books. David Bellamy, patron of the reserve, was a friend and admired her spirit and energy as well as enjoying her legendary hospitality.

He described her as *"a powerhouse of drive and energy"* Wetlands 1990

The Norfolk Naturalists' Trust and Norfolk and Norwich Naturalists' Society awarded her their top honour, a Sidney Long medal, in 1997, for her services to nature conservation in Norfolk.

Our mother was a strong and remarkable woman with a fascinating life story.

We hope that this book will appeal to both those who knew and admired Phyllis as well as introducing her to new readers.

The Ellis Family

"She had a marvellous command of the English language and could take the opposition apart at a meeting"

Dr Roy Baker UEA

From the Editor

I had the pleasure of working with Phyllis for several years on her reminiscences. I cycled over to see her about once a week for a cup of tea and an hour or so of conversation and stories which I recorded on tape.

Life was vivid to Phyllis... both in the present and in the past. Our chats were great fun. But since I finished putting the account together, other members of her family have put in a lot of work, checking and comparing dates. By and large, they confirmed that she had an excellent memory. But I'd like to thank them. The book, as a result, is very much a team effort... and all the better for it.

Pete Kelley

Phyllis' Family Tree

Parents	Grandparents	Great Grandparents

John
Chambers
1857–1925

Edward
Chambers
Born 1832

Clara
Hinton
Born 1832

John
Debenham
Chambers
1884–1962

Thomas
William
Debenham
Born 1822

Lucy
Rebecca
Debenham
1858–1942

Phyllis Ellis

Lucy
Algar
Born 1815

Phyllis
Mary
Chambers
1913–2004

William
Land
1828-1878

Edwin Land
1860–1937

Mary
Stebbings
1830-1929

Ada Land
1883–1938

Jeremiah
Whitlock
Born 1806

Eliza
Whitlock
1854–1938

Jemima
Brockway
Born 1807

Chapter 1

"On both sides of the family you had this sharp memory of independence of spirit!"

ANCESTORS

What did you do after supper, with only a paraffin lamp and candles? The light wasn't good enough, you see, to read by an awful lot. Well, you went visiting. You played cards. Without television and radio, you talked. So you had an awful lot of history being passed down by word of mouth to the young in the 1920s.

In this way, I learned that my grandfather, John Chambers, was born at Quinton, near Birmingham, the only son of Edward – a man who owned mines, or was a partner in mines – in that area.

Now, Edward's father, John senior, was a well-known character in Birmingham, very dominant – an industrious man who was also founding superintendent of Quinton Primitive Methodist Sunday School, and its secretary and treasurer for many years. He was public-spirited, and got the first public lavatories built in Birmingham, but he was frequently involved in lawsuits, fighting county councils and corporations over rights of way. Consequently, when he died there was very little money left.

Great-grandfather's own father – or possibly grandfather – had been an iron founder, and travelled the country with his wagon and horses, carrying a mobile forge. He came to Blythburgh when the mill was built there, and cast an iron millwheel – one of the earliest. It took him three days to get there from Birmingham, and three days going back again.

The Chambers family still had, in those days, a house and two acres at Quinton which had been given to them about 1483, in fief, by the Earl of Warwick, a reward for an ancestor's services, fighting in Ireland.

My father's mother was Lucy Rebecca Debenham, and her family had lived in Debenham for over seven centuries.

So, you see, on both sides, my father's family were independently-minded people. Both my grandfathers had the consciousness that they were... as good as the next people. When you know your family have been in a certain place for centuries, well, you have a history at the back of you. You have a certain pride in your family... a feeling of continuity.

On Mother's side, the Lands, her father's family, were a Norfolk family. My great-grandfather Land originally came from North Norfolk, but he had gone to work for Queen Victoria at Osborne House on the Isle of Wight, becoming the Queen's head gamekeeper. Game-keeping is a profession said to go back for generations in the Land family.

Grandmother was Eliza Whitlock. Her father had been a successful dairy farmer, in Hampshire, living in a big house, sending his milk to London on the train. His children were sent to private schools. However, he didn't own the land he farmed. It was rented, as was common at that time. His whole herd got cow pox and, with no government compensation, he was reduced to poverty, lost everything. He became a gardener to the rector, and presumably lived in one of the rector's cottages.

So on both sides of the family, you had this strong memory of independence of spirit, of yeomen. It can be extraordinarily difficult, because you can create a feeling that you're being bossy and criticising all the time, when you're not. You are just being... I suppose, a leader.

One has to take a risk... this is another thing about the upbringing, that you are willing to take what seems a good risk at times.

Anyhow, returning to my ancestors...

My grandfather Chambers – in Quinton – probably had rather a hard childhood. He was the only son, and I think his father was quite strict. Grandfather decided he would teach. He trained at Quinton College, and was one of the early certificated teachers. He came to Bungay for his first job. There he met Lucy, a milliner. When they were courting, her mother used to follow behind them with a big stick hidden in her skirt, in case he tried any funny-business.

Lucy had been born not far away, at Diss. I remember her telling me the garden of the house went down to the Mere, though we've never been able to identify it. She said she used to have to watch the geese as a child, sitting on the steps of the staithe at the bottom of their garden. Lucy was the seventh daughter of a seventh daughter – a very mystical position. Certainly she was inclined to have dreams which foretold happenings. Though it seems hard to believe now, she actually stopped some people from going on the Titanic because she was convinced – because of a dream – that it would sink.

Another time, during the First World War, she dreamed about a dirigible that came down. They went to the spot next morning, and found it. The two Germans are buried nearby. She had... a tremendous sense of danger. I can only call it that.

Anyhow, her family had left Diss when Lucy was about six and by seven she was a pupil at a Dame School in Bungay, where she and her sisters had what was called 'An Education' in those days. Every afternoon, they had to sit wearing backboards, to keep their backs straight, and do cross-stitch samplers while they were being trained to sit up straight.

Lucy and John were married at St Mary's Church, Bungay, and soon after he became the master at Wenhaston, a small school, at £17 a quarter. It was at Wenhaston that my father, Jack, was born on January 9th. I believe the year was 1884, since he was a year younger than my mother.

Now, at Wenhaston, my grandfather was paid by the Lady of the Manor. He had to go up once a quarter for his pay cheque. One quarter's day, he went as usual and the Lady said: "Well, Chambers, I've decided that if I pay you once a year, it'll save me money." At that time, you had to pay for every cheque you drew. Now, my grandfather was a fiery man and I'm afraid he told her straight that that would not be convenient, and that he required his quarter's pay then, there and at once.

Soon after, he got a better job as the master at Benhall. It was a very large, very poor village and had a lot of large families. So it was a big school for a village – with around 140 children. But Grandfather was in his element there, and stayed there for the rest of his life.

Returning to Grandma Land – then little Eliza Whitlock – she had a difficult childhood, as the youngest of 13 children. By the time she was born, her eldest sister – and possibly two of them – were married with their own children, and she always indicated that her mother had been quite an old lady. I believe Grandma was brought up virtually as an only child.

She was about nine when her father lost his herd. After that, Eliza's private education ended, and she went to the village school – riding there with the coachman's daughter, and swapping sandwiches with her. Eliza always had ham sandwiches. The coachman's daughter only got mustard. But Eliza preferred the mustard sandwiches.

To help the family income, after the disaster, her own mother went and did catering, when there were parties or dinners with lots of guests at 'the big house' – whether Grandma meant the rectory or the hall, I don't know.

I remember her giving me a recipe for savoury eggs which they had at the dinner. After all your soups... and fish... and game... and meat... and water ices... then your sweet... followed by cheese... you then had these savoury eggs. After which, presumably, you wanted something for your indigestion!

Anyway, despite her family's fallen circumstances, Eliza was well-educated – it is assumed, partly at home. She could write a good hand, could converse on a wide range of subjects, and became an expert needlewoman. So, on leaving school, she got a job with Lady Agar in London, making clothes for her eleven children and for the Lady, and knitting silk socks for the whole family.

I remember she had an amazing collection of crests from envelopes that she had collected when they were being thrown away. She also had a collection of the most lovely greetings cards, with embroidered muslin on them, that she had mounted in big scrapbooks.

It was the time of bouffant sleeves, tight cuffs, bustles at the back and trailing skirts, but she had the ability to go into Hyde Park and follow a fashionable dress – no doubt dashing round by another path to see it from the front – then go home, draw it and – if the lady liked it – buy the material, cut it out and make it. When she eventually left to marry my grandfather, the Agars told her in no uncertain terms that if she wasn't happy, she should come back!

Now, as I have said, Eliza's future husband, Edwin Land, grew up on the Isle of Wight where his father, William, was head gamekeeper. Edwin had been born in Norfolk, however, about 1860 – before his own father left to work initially for Earl Cowper in Hertfordshire, and eventually for Queen Victoria. Edwin was the oldest of five children.

Queen Victoria dominated the island and Grandfather, as a young man, found it very trying that whenever the Queen passed by, outriders travelled half a mile ahead, even on the Isle of Wight, which is very small. Any men along the roadside – the 'peasants', so to speak – had to stand with their hats off every time (rain, snow or whatever), ready to bow while the women stood ready to curtsy as the coach went by. Well, Grandfather – if he heard the coach in the distance – would just go into the handiest ditch and hide until it went past!

Edwin was only 18 when, in 1878, his father died relatively young – aged about 46. Queen Victoria chose the grave site, at Whippingham church, and personally attended the funeral on the Tuesday before April 5th 1878 with Princess Beatrice and a number of other dignitaries.

The Queen then installed Great-grandma and the young family in Coburg Cottage, to look after it. As the oldest son, Grandfather was taken on as the lowliest form of game-keeper, a kennel boy. Despite its name, the 'cottage' was an enormous house where Queen Victoria kept a suite of rooms to which she retired when she got fed up with all the protocol.

I remember Great-grandma clearly. She didn't die until 1921, when she was 91. She was very stiff and starchy... probably stiffer and starchier than the Royal Family!

Now, Queen Victoria kept a strict eye on her servants in all respects. If you were an employee, you had to ask her permission to marry, and ask for a cottage. But Grandfather, shortly after his father's death and before he was quite 20, married Eliza and somehow found himself a cottage without asking royal permission. So he got the order of the boot – pronto! That, I have always been told, is why he was sacked.

Grandfather was out of work for a while. Later he was asked several times, by George V, to go back into royal service, but he always refused. He said he'd had enough of that.

An article dated July 1901 in '*The Gamekeeper*' magazine charts his next few years. Edwin worked as under-secretary on Stockgrove Estate, in Bedfordshire. Two years later, he moved to Yorkshire, on Farnley Hall Estate, then back to Stockgrove after another two as head keeper, staying for seven years, then a similar post at Crowboro Warren Estate, Sussex. After two years there, his employer died and he began working for a Mr Wood at Exbury Estate in Hampshire.

It was Mr Wood's decision to purchase Sudbourne Hall Estate, in Suffolk, three years later – in the mid 1890s –

that brought Edwin's family to the estate where I knew my grandparents, for Grandfather moved with his employer.

Mother was born on 18th January 1883.

At one stage, Grandfather worked for Baron de Ville, owner of a champagne company and very wealthy. I was told it was while working for Baron de Ville that Grandfather was shot by poachers. My grandmother had become very worried by two in the morning, and went out – leaving the children asleep – to search for him. She found him badly injured and left for dead. They had a telephone, even in those early days, so the baron called out the hospital ambulance.

Grandfather was taken in, and eventually recovered. However, when I knew him, he had a glass eye. He had lost his right eye. Whether he lost it that night, or at some other time in an accident with his gun, I don't know, but Grandfather was an absolute crack shot, and he always told me he put it down to having only one eye... and not having to close the other when he fired.

After the baron died, my grandparents hit a bad patch. The baroness sold up, and moved to London.

As a small child, I remember going to visit her in a magnificent Victorian flat at West End Mansions on the Finchley Road. There was a wonderful lavatory with a wooden seat, a china bowl with a blue willow-pattern design in the bottom, and a handle at the side that you could pull to flush it.

Grandfather was out of work for some time again, after the estate was sold. When he was 18, he had grown a beard to make himself look older. By this time, he must have been in his 30s, so he cut the beard off to make himself look younger – and eventually got a job with Mr Wood, who was involved with the Wallace art collection.

After Mr Wood moved to Suffolk, Grandfather never looked back. It was a lifetime's job. There were 30 keepers, one for each 1,000 acres. It was at that time the biggest shooting estate in Suffolk.

Mother had, I should think, just about left school when they came to Sudbourne. She would have left school at 14 – that is, in 1897. She was the elder daughter; she had a sister, Ella, six years younger.

Mother went to work at Benhall School at 15, in about 1898 – originally, I suppose, as a pupil-teacher. But she was made to study and went to night classes at Saxmundham, two miles away. I think she lived at the Chambers' house.

I know Mother said that Grandfather went out one day, leaving her in charge. The sliding room-dividers were pushed back, and she was in charge of 80 children. She had a spot of bother with them throwing ink pellets. Then Grandfather came back and saw all this mess. So he said: "Everyone who threw ink pellets, stand in front." Practically the whole class walked to the front. He went up and down the line twice with a cane, and no more trouble was had.

At that time, my father would have been nearly 15, too. But he had already gone to London to train as a post office clerk in Waltham Cross, where Grandfather Land's sister, Sarah, was married to the postmaster. So, you had this extraordinary situation – that the son of one family was going to relatives of the other family, whose daughter was coming as a pupil-teacher to the first family. The two families had presumably met up because Grandfather Land used to sometimes ride over to Benhall.

So, my parents' courting must have been done in holiday times, when Mother went to visit her aunt Sarah or when Father came back to stay with his parents. They didn't get to see a lot of each other before they were married in 1909. My father – a year younger – was 25. I have a photograph of my mother's wedding festivities, which included a whist drive on the front grass.

Jack and Ada's Wedding Breakfast Whist Drive, Sudbourne, 1910

Benhall School 1907 (postcard sent by Ada to Jack)

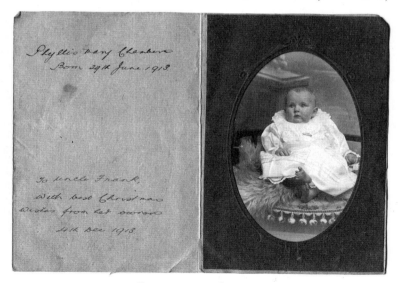

Christmas card of baby Phyllis sent to Jack's brother
Frank in 1913 'from her owners'

Grandfather John Chambers, the headmaster at Benhall School 1912 wearing suit, shirt and socks made by his wife Lucy Rebecca

Chapter 2

'It's very fresh in my memory – all the fun'

CHILDHOOD

You know, I was watching people in the street, and often, they go along, looking at things. They're not smiling... or, largely, even talking to each other. Sad, rather solemn faces. They don't look as though they are interested in anything. In my childhood, everything was of interest, and we had such a lot of laughter in the house.

Grandfather John Chambers was schoolmaster at Benhall. Very short legs and a long body. He'd run like the wind. Used to chase his own truants, jump hedges and dykes.

He was a churchwarden, an organist... you name it. Life was very full, and so much fun. I can see us now, sitting back after the evening meal and Grandad Chambers reciting a funny poem or recounting something which had happened. There was always something amusing, even if he got in a temper and chased somebody round the table with a hairbrush – which he often did when the children were young – it all ended in laughter. There were never any recriminations.

And there was always so much music. Grandad's favourite instrument was the viola, which he usually played when his friends came. I remember, at seven, with three or four other people in the room playing instruments, being sat on the piano stool and screwed up to the right height, and told: "Well, you can get on and if you get lost just wait until you pick us up." That was how I learned to sight-read. They were all good-tempered about it.

And there was always a dictionary on the table. Knowing what you were saying, what you were talking about, and using the language properly... and how to spell words. Your vocabulary was always increasing.

Before Grandfather came, Benhall had been a rigid 'Three Rs' sort of school, whereas he believed in teaching country children country things. Grandfather became a friend of the local squire, and was given complete freedom... as a result he feared no man. That's right. That's also what the old coachman said to Ted, when he first went to work at Keswick, when he was 16: "Fear no man. FEAR... NO... MAN!" And they didn't, any of them. You did your best to be pleasant, but you didn't 'kow-tow'.

This, too, was part of the reason for the dictionary on the table: to know what you were talking about.

You see, although my father and his brother Frank never went to college and although they left school at 14, they had a remarkable command of the English language. They could write an extremely good letter. If they read something from a lawyer, they knew what they were reading.

Grandfather Chambers always tried to interest the children at school in words. And he insisted on a lot of singing... starting with nursery rhymes, and working up the scale. His school usually won the East Suffolk prize for the best choir each year.

I don't know that Grandma played anything, but she sang and had a beautiful voice. She was still singing at 84. My grandparents started an operatic society at Saxmundham, which was two miles away, and every year they put on some sort of production... with Grandma usually as the heroine and Grandad, with his short legs, probably as the villain.

I have a picture of them with my father – who was then 12 – dressed up for Gilbert and Sullivan. And, of course, if you do *The Yeoman of the Guard* or *The Mikado*, then you are going to have a tremendous input into your vocabulary. Even just a popular song like '*Come Into The Garden Maud*' with the line '*... the black bat night has flown*'. Think of that – a wonderful expression!

Then, I was brought up with the Bible. Grandfather read the lessons at church, and we'd always got hymns. So it was all an expansion... from nursery rhymes up... not to more 'worthwhile' music, but to songs with a bigger vocabulary.

Music was his great thing. He could play practically any instrument he laid his hands on. He took the church organ to bits, tuned it and put it back together again... and I'm not talking about a small organ. Apart from the viola, he played the violin and, as he grew older, in his spare time he made violins.

He also composed hymn tunes and psalms.

My father learned the violin as a boy. When I was a child, the... the Daily Mail, I think it was... used to have a piece of music in every week: '*Coal Black Mammy of Mine*' and things like that. The latest jazz. This would be 1917 or 1918, and Grandad used to play these pieces on the church organ as voluntaries, just augmenting them and altering them slightly for fun.

Grandfather was the only son of an only son, and all his father's tools had come down to him. As a child, he allowed me the run of his tool shed when he was there... watching him turn things on the lathe. I was always welcome there, and allowed a piece of wood and to handle the tools, to treadle the lathe and turn things myself. I can't have been more than seven.

An extraordinary character. Poor Grandad. I was only 11 when he died, but it's very fresh in my memory – all the fun we had.

My father, Jack, was still a baby in arms when my grandparents came to Benhall... coming into this very much larger house than they'd been used to, and a larger school. It was a thatched house, very old, and had once been an inn.

Benhall was one of the poorest villages in Suffolk, with more than its share of social problems. But Grandfather became a great friend of the local squire, Mr Holland, who proved to have a strong interest in education, and responded positively to Grandfather's enthusiasm and ideas.

My grandfather was, I think, one of the first schoolmasters to have a school garden. He realised that people needed help learning to grow vegetables. So Mr Holland gave the school a meadow, which Grandfather turned partly into a playing field and partly into an allotment.

People have such romantic ideas about cottage gardens, and how picturesque the villages were, but the truth is that the people were very poor. I don't think they did much more than keep a pig at the bottom, grow a few potatoes and cabbages. I don't believe in these pictures you see of cottages surrounded by lovely flowers. They were certainly not in the villages of my childhood.

Another thing Grandfather did, which earned him opprobrium from the farmers, was to teach the fathers of his children to use a chain to measure pieces of land accurately. You see, it was a village that had a lot of odd corners. You'd have a nice piece of land that was long on one side, or triangular or had a round curve at the top. And a farmer would put one of these pightles of land down to swedes for the cattle (not sugar beet, in those days), and say: "Well, Jack ... call it an acre and a half." And the man would be paid at piece-work rates, you see.

Well, my grandfather would go along and say: "That's not an acre and a half: that's two acres." And he'd get his chain out and measure it. In the end, he held an evening class, taught the men how to use the chain and calculate areas for themselves.

He was very independent.

I'm told he was the so-called 'plotter' who started the first teachers' strike at Lowestoft. I'm not sure of the year, but this would be prior to 1917. Perhaps 1916. Teachers, you see, were very badly paid before 1917. You had payment by results, so if you had children of lesser learning ability, the teacher suffered.

Grandfather wasn't well off. He had quite large classes, and quite a lot of children who were difficult to teach. Children could leave at 12 if they could read, write and do their arithmetic. But he had a lot of children staying until 14, and then leaving still unable to read or write.

His own house had an enormous garden, which was his pride and joy. He adored gardening, and set it out with big asparagus beds and vegetable plots. At the bottom of that was the school garden, with little box hedges all the way round. He taught the children to grow Brussels sprouts and other vegetables, to prune fruit bushes properly and –

of course – he included a flower garden. He taught them to look after and bud roses.

A school inspector later published the first book on school gardening, inscribed 'with thanks to Mr John Chambers'. In actual fact, the book was largely my grandfather's work.

My grandparents immersed themselves in village life, and Grandfather spent the rest of his career there – turning down several opportunities to move to larger schools, including the headship of Church Road Schools at Gorleston when they were first built – big, modern buildings, enormous for those days.

He did go and take a look but – much to my grandmother's disappointment, I think – he decided it was too much like town. He preferred the country. Grandma, I think, would have enjoyed being in town.

At home, there were two back-doors. One was the 'club back-door', where he ran a club for boys to come and learn to do a bit of carpentry. So Grandfather had a very 'open' attitude. He didn't treat school as something separate from everyday life. He took education out into the village, too.

As for Grandma, well... she was living in a poor village with a husband who thought nothing of giving away half his salary at times. And with all these people around her, she, too, was driven to help.

She ran a weekly sewing party. She was the only woman in the village with a sewing machine, and she and Grandfather had bicycles. It was two miles to Saxmundham, so she used to go into Saxmundham to buy calico at one penny a yard, and other cheap material. Village women came to her house, and she taught them to make their own clothes.

My grandmother made all her own children's clothes, and all my grandfather's clothes – including his suits. He used to boast that she made everything except his boots. My poor grandmother... she said she never knew when she would have a child at the door, asking could they have Frankie's spare shoes or Jack's old trousers. I think she fed them, often, too.

I think Grandad must have been a very tough schoolmaster, but he was well thought of and very generous. He couldn't bear to see children without shoes.

The other back-door led to the place where Grandma kept her blue-flame oil stove for cooking, then through a long, narrow kitchen into a third kitchen where the hand sink was. All the water was carried through in buckets from outside the back-door, where both my grandmothers had huge tubs – taller than me – which held gallons and gallons of rainwater, and had a tap at the bottom. At Benhall, the tub collected water off the side roof, which was tiled. So you made the washing water last.

Drinking water came from even further away – a 90-foot well, shared with a little wooden cottage, which was quite a walk through the garden.

In a room upstairs, there were two round windows through which they could see down the Saxmundham road towards London – so that, when the house had been an inn, they could watch for coaches coming, and get warming pans out for the beds, get food on the way and so on.

Pieces of glass were rescued from one of those round windows in which Ireton, one of Cromwell's generals, had scratched his name with a diamond ring.

The Scopes lived in the wooden cottage –'Old Man Scopes', who was a farm labourer, and Harriet, his daughter, who used to help in my grandparents' house sometimes. There was no Mrs Scopes, in those days. Their cottage was just one room down, and two tiny rooms upstairs. There was a great big cobnut tree in the yard, with a seat under it. Old Man Scopes used to sit on this seat, on a Sunday, when it was fine, and you could hear him reading the paper to himself. Every now and again, there would be a pause and "HAARD WAARD!" He used to say "HAARD WAARD!" whenever he got to a word of more than two syllables.

In his class, Grandad had one boy who was very clever – the son of a widow. When he was 12, he passed all the tests to leave school, and a farmer – a rather brutal man – wanted the boy to come and work for him. But Grandad thought he was worthy of better things. So he got him an interview with a lawyer in Saxmundham. The boy went to the interview dressed in all my father's clothes – his best jacket and best overcoat. Probably his best shoes, as well. He went on to become a successful lawyer.

At one time, my grandfather was borrowing a horse and cart from a farmer, once a week, so he could travel to Leiston, where he ran an evening class.

Along with Jack, my father, my grandparents had two other children – Frank, who became an engineer, and Claire, who became a teacher and headmistress.

Until he had heart trouble, Grandad Chambers had been a very strong man, as his father was. Unfortunately, he had angina and, eventually, Bright's disease. So he retired at 60, and became agent on Benhall Estate for Mr Holland, the squire, who was also the parson. There, he made plans for new cottages and improvements.

Grandad died when he was 64, when I was only 11, but – you know – I've such vivid memories of him – a man of great energy, all the fun we had, a man interested in the gardening side of nature, with the American organ in the parlour and the piano in the living room, going to church to hear him play the organ or read the lesson. Tremendous zest for living.

After he died, in 1924, things altered a lot for me. There was no going to Benhall any more. In 1928, Grandma Chambers moved to Halesworth, then a small country town, where she lived for about 20 years. I spent a lot of holidays there. It was nice. There was a narrow-gauge railway running all the way to Southwold, with two or three little stations on the way. The steam engine had a dragon on the front. I believe the railway had been made for the Emperor of Japan. The carriages were like trams, and you sat facing one another on wooden seats.

The first stop was Holton Corner, where I had some friends. They had a farm, and the railway went across at the back of the farm-house. When we took the cows across, we always had to have a railway timetable handy!

At Halesworth, everyone had a wireless with a tall aerial out the back. If you 'jiffled' your wireless from one station to another, it made all the other wirelesses in the road make horrible noises. My Uncle Frank balanced a piece of wire on top of his aerial so, if he found people in the road were changing their station too often, he used to go out and tug the wire – which upset all the other sets. He was very naughty... quite wicked!

Grandma Chambers could knit, crochet, embroider, tat.
My mother had taught her to knit in 1914, when they were
all busy knitting things for the soldiers. And after the war,
Grandmother used to be sent wool from the Dr Barnado's
Homes. Every week of her life, she knitted two pairs of
socks for Dr Barnado's. She'd still got some on the knitting
pins when she died.

John Chambers and Lucy Rebecca Debenham 1857

John Chambers and Lucy Rebecca Chambers 1912

Jack and Ada 1910

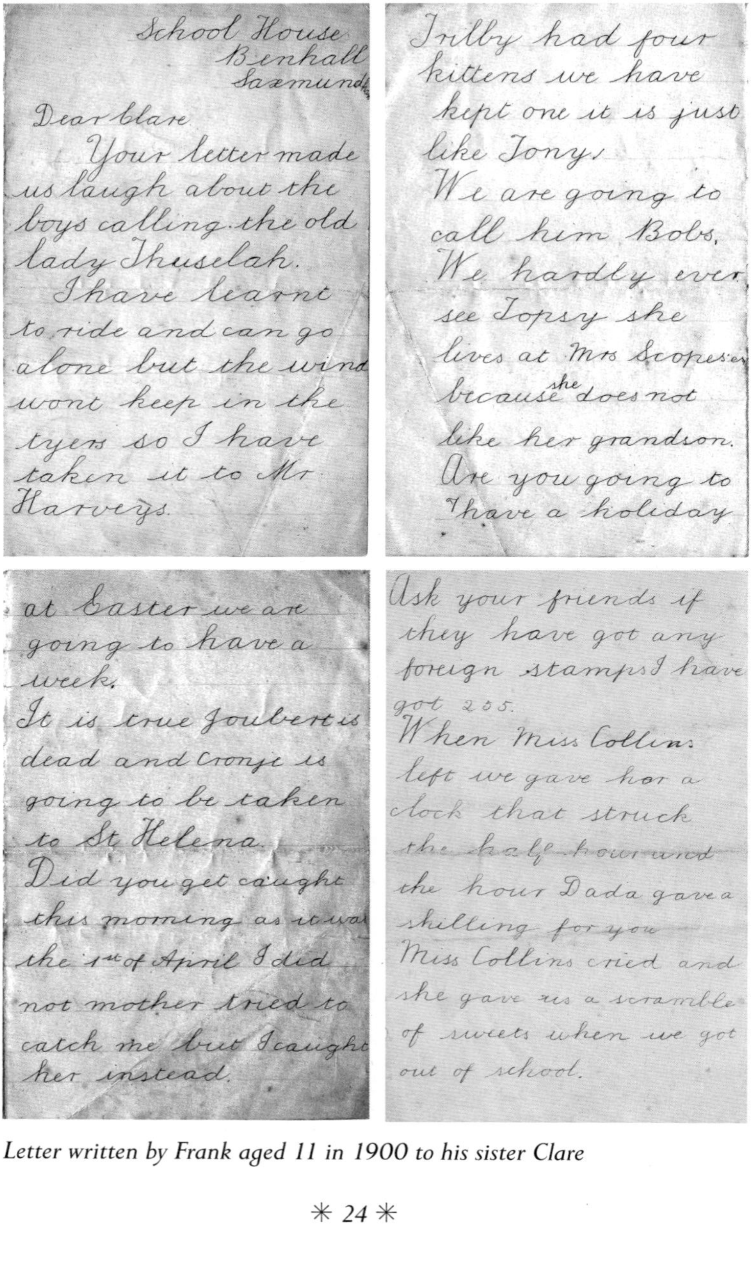

School House
Benhall
Saxmundham

Dear Clare

Your letter made us laugh about the boys calling the old lady Thuselah.

I have learnt to ride and can go alone but the wind wont keep in the tyers so I have taken it to Mr Harveys.

Trilby had four kittens we have kept one it is just like Tony.

We are going to call him Bobs.

We hardly ever see Topsy she lives at Mrs Scopes because she does not like her grandson.

Are you going to I have a holiday

at Easter we are going to have a week.

It is true Joubert is dead and Cronje is going to be taken to St Helena.

Did you get caught this morning as it was the 1st of April I did not mother tried to catch me but I caught her instead.

Ask your friends if they have got any foreign stamps I have got 205.

When Miss Collins left we gave her a clock that struck the half hour and the hour Dada gave a shilling for you Miss Collins cried and she gave us a scramble of sweets when we got out of school.

Letter written by Frank aged 11 in 1900 to his sister Clare

Benhall School House circa 1890

*Three generations of
Chambers circa 1894*

left to right

*back row: Grandfather John
Chambers, Jack Chambers,
Great Grandfather Edward
Chambers*

*mid row: Great Great Aunt
Anne Dimmack, Clare
Chambers, Grandmother
Lucy Chambers*

front: Frank Chambers

Grandfather John Chambers with Clare circa 1890

Operatic Society, John, Lucy and Jack (other unknown) circa 1894

Sudbourne Hall 1901 (licensed for reproduction from Country Life Magazine)

Ada & Phyllis 1914 (the game-keeper's daughter and grandchild)

Ada and Phyllis 1914. This picture went to war in Jack's pocket.

* 28 *

Chapter Three

*"When we got to Sudbourne Hall I was allowed
the run of the place"*

EARLY YEARS

I was born in Yarmouth on June 29th 1913. My parents had
rented a house in Palgrave Road, but I was only 18 months
old when my father, Jack, was sent abroad – to France – as a
soldier.

By the time the war began, we were living in Northgate
Street. Mother was another very independent character.
In the early days of their marriage, she had found that
Father was over-generous. He would be paid on a Friday
night, and would lend money – or even give it away – before
he got home. So she used to go down on a Friday night
and meet him... ready to do the shopping while he still
had the money. That was Mother all over – take action
when necessary.

She had enjoyed teaching, but did not work after she was
married. Still, she was a good cook and a friendly woman,
and even before I was born she was taking in lodgers, as
everyone did in that part of Yarmouth.

Father was 30, and a clerk in the post office, but when the
war started, he volunteered. It was early January in 1915.
I was too young to miss him, of course. Yarmouth was being
bombarded from the sea and, with Father away, Mother
went home to her parents at Sudbourne, in Suffolk,

Ada and Jack 1914

So it is at Sudbourne that I have one of my earliest memories... of a Zeppelin.

The mail was taken every morning from Orford post office at 2am in a horse-drawn van to Wickham Market station. One night, we were woken up by a man banging on Grandfather's door, shouting and shouting: "Mr Land! Mr Land! Come down! Wake up! They're arter me!" It was the poor postman. His van was being followed by a dirigible, which was obviously following his light, hoping it would lead the pilot to the railway, so he could drop his bombs. He was mortally terrified.

My grandfather shouted out of the window: "Dowse your light, you fool... and be quick about it!"

So he did. Then we all came down, including me. And once all the lights were out – no candles or anything – I suppose there must have been still a bit of moonlight, because I remember watching the dirigible stop right overhead. It paused and a little trapdoor opened. We could see this man looking down, trying to discover where he was. Eventually, he gave up and went away. To me, it was very exciting.

I had been christened at Sudbourne. I have a silver inkstand which marks the date. I imagine there was a big party, because I was the only granddaughter, and we were a churchgoing family. We went to church every Sunday... about a mile's walk from the house. My grandfather didn't go. Just the women. Though he did go to services on special occasions.

After we went to Sudbourne, Mother began teaching at Orford School. They were glad of a woman teacher because all the men had gone to war. Grandma was already over

60 so, at three-and-a-half, I went to school with Mother... in one of those white pinafores with lace around it. Styles hadn't changed very much. I've got photographs of Mother, as a young child, dressed in just the same way.

Well, the first day, Mother took me on the carrier of her bicycle but the Clarks' car came by. (They were the family that lived at the Hall.) I was so frightened that I fell off. I'd never seen a car before.

After that I insisted on walking. So I used to walk across the woods alone, accompanied by two dogs. Grandfather insisted I take the dogs. Other children brought dogs, too, and there were kennels at the school to put them in. In those days, your parents got you there by hook or by crook, and everyone was too busy to take their children to school, especially in the country. One child came on a donkey.

There must have been all of 25-50 children in that class – from young juniors down to infants with desks at various levels. It was quite a big school, with another class of older juniors and, through the door from the infants' classroom, two more classes – younger seniors and older seniors. By that time, I think, they were leaving school at 14, not 12 any more.

Anyway, I was given a tray with sand to do pictures with, a slate, a slate pencil and a rubber.

I remember there was a girl sitting next to me and I was absolutely fascinated, watching all these little animals running around on her head. She had nits. They sent her home, where her head was shaved. After that, she was given a three-legged stool to sit on by herself, away from the others. Poor child! The dreadful things they did!

I hadn't been at school long before I had impetigo and because, in those days, it was supposed to be a 'dirty' disease, Mother tried to cope with it on her own. I remember being in bed in what was called the Spare Bedroom. You could look right across country and see the sea, watch the boats. Because the war was on, there was a lot of traffic along the coast and plenty to see.

But before I was four, we moved to Sudbourne Hall to live with Mrs Clark.

Mrs Clark was alone and wanted someone to talk to. Her husband had taken his yacht to the north of Scotland, patrolling for submarines, at about the time of the Battle of Jutland. They had one son, Kenneth – later the same Sir Kenneth Clark who wrote '*Civilisation*'. But then he was away at school, and only came home for holidays.

So Mrs Clark was 'alone' – that is, apart from the butler, Mrs Troke the housekeeper, the lady's maid, a cook and at least one kitchen maid, Mr Pryke the coachman, several gardeners... oh, and there was the chauffeur. But she was 'alone'. Well, I suppose she felt she couldn't confabulate with the servants.

Mother, my Aunt Ella and Grandma were not considered to be servants, but rather they were 'companions'. Remember, my grandmother had had a good education. She had been brought up in a big house, at first, until her father was ruined. She could talk. She knew a lot. She was widely read. She was quite capable of taking her needlework, and chatting with Mrs Clark or playing cards. And every afternoon, they would go and play golf on the private, nine-hole course there.

So we went with Grandmother to live in these rather splendid surroundings. We, of course, lived in the servants' quarters, but they were still very luxurious compared to what we were used to. There was electric light, hot and cold running water, a flush lavatory, a bathroom.

The main part of the Hall was three or four storeys high, with magnificent bathrooms. One marvellous room had peacock wallpaper, with curtains to match. Even the china on the wash-stand matched the wallpaper – all beautiful red, blue, green and gold peacocks and flowers.

There was a big hall with curved windows that looked out onto a terrace and a rose garden, and down to what we called 'The Lake', though it wasn't very big. The Lake was wonderful in Spring, with a pure belt of pheasant's eye narcissi. Even now, I can see this sheet of gleaming-white narcissi with their little orangey-red eyes, and the marvellous scent that wafted from them! Oh, the smell was wonderful!

The Hall had a lovely collection of stuffed birds, including a heron on a stand in a glass case. There was also a rocking chair with red velvet on it. I discovered that, if you rocked, the heron on the stand rocked, too!

Then there was a library I could explore and part of it was a collection of children's books... Peter Pan, a lot of Edwardian stories. There was also an enormous, old-fashioned car with huge headlights sitting up from it, perhaps a Packard. I never rode in a car until 1926, when the General Strike was on. I was terrified of them.

In the place where the car was kept – and, to me, equally fascinating – there was also a big brass engine going round all the time. In my memory, it was huge – and rather frightening – with lots of batteries. It was an electricity generator, and served the whole Hall, the cottages and the living quarters around.

I remember when my aunt Ella had an operation, the doctor came and performed it at the Hall. She had a lump in her side. I remember smelling the chloroform from outside the door, and then going in and being shown this lump... purple and red and shiny. Extraordinary thing to show a child, but it didn't frighten me. I was just interested. Well, I was used to seeing dead birds, rabbits and so on.

Grandad Land had a pony and trap. I used to go round the whole estate when I wasn't at school. Grandfather also hated making up the books. So, as soon as I could write properly and read, which was very early, before I was four, I made up the game books and pay books every week for the keepers that were left: Nash, Kersey, Caley, England... and another one down near Iken whose name I don't know. By the time the war had been on for a year, he'd only got five of the original 30. The rest had been called up.

There was also a warrener and a rat catcher, who got 4d – four old pence – a rabbit, and a penny for a rat's tail.

Anyhow, when we got to the Hall, I was allowed the run of the place. I remember my father sent me a pair of roller-skates from abroad, and I skated up and down these long corridors paved in black and white marble tesserae. I'm afraid the butler had to beware, if he was carrying glasses!

And in the big, bay-windowed hall, which was also a minstrels' gallery, there was an ENORMOUS grand piano. I couldn't leave it alone! When Mrs Clark noticed this, she said "She'd better learn!" and summoned Olive Gould to come in and teach me twice a week. I was possibly only three-and-a-half. Olive taught at the tiny Sudbourne School and lived at The Chequers Inn, Sudbourne, where her father was the landlord.

My first three years at school seemed to be mainly occupied with being ill – whooping cough, mumps, impetigo – so I was at home a lot. The servants were very good to me, but there were no other children to play with...so the piano became my toy.

And once lessons started, I had to practise. They wouldn't let me touch the piano unless I practised properly. So I did. It was something to do, you see. Until your fingers get used to the keyboard, you've got to keep up practice every day, until your fingers recognise the spacing without thought.

There was always music in the Land family. Grandma Land played the concertina, and mother had learned the violin – though she stopped playing before I was born. Her sister, Ella, played the piano. So, what with being pushed at one end, and going to stay with my other grandparents, the Chambers, who were even more musical... well, it was necessary for me to know what I was looking at. Hence my ability to sight-read.

There were always big wood fires, and there was singing in the evenings when any of the family was home or when anyone came to the house. By the time I was six, I could play for a sing-song.

At Sudbourne Hall, too, we always had a lot of music – friends coming in. In the winter, we would have a fire in the parlour and sit around the piano to sing. We entertained the men from the hospital sometimes – the 'walking

wounded' sent home from the war. They would be given
tea and sandwiches, and we would sing '*It's A Long Way to
Tipperary*' or '*There's A Long, Long Trail A-Winding*'.

Oh, I had a lot of fun, you know.

They also had a pianola in the billiard room. When young
Kenneth came back from school, on holiday, we used to
go through the pianola rolls. And he'd take me out in a boat
on The Lake. It was extraordinary, a boy of 14 spending his
time with a four-year-old girl, but he was always different from
other people and perhaps, like me, a lonely child. He wasn't
very happy at that time. He didn't like shooting – which, of
course, annoyed his father, and he would never go out with
the shooting parties.

Young Kenneth used to get very upset when all these birds
were brought in – pheasants and ducks. They looked so
beautiful in their winter plumage, and to see all these
hundreds of birds hanging on hooks in the Game Room.

It didn't upset me a bit. I thought about what they tasted
like, not what they looked like! Well, I suppose I was more
used to it. Even at that early age, I had helped to pluck
birds when we were at Smokey House, and there was always
skinning and gutting going on, at least once a day.

I had whooping cough very badly. I think I was off school
for three months. Dr Baron used to come from Orford in
his high collar and frock coat. Terrible medicine! Pink,
and very salt. I can taste it now. In the end, Mother took
me to Clacton... to Great Aunt Sarah, Grandad Land's sister.

I remember being taken onto the beach, and told to
breathe the salt air from the rocks, which had seaweed all
over them. The ozone was supposed to be good for me.

Whether they actually took me to the gasworks, I can't remember. But that was supposed to be the other cure for whooping cough – to go around the gasworks and inhale the coke fumes.

Very different from modern medicine, isn't it?

Great Aunt Sarah was very Victorian, and had a boarding house. So there were 12 of us sitting around the table. As a child, I was served last and I remember being terribly worried when she served the pudding out – seeing all these helpings going out around the big table – and wondering if there was going to be any left for me at the end.

I suppose, in those days, I must have had good manners. Otherwise, they wouldn't have had me at the table. They'd have fed me in the kitchen.

I don't remember my father until 1917. He came home on a week's leave. He was so infested with lice that my mother made him strip off on the doorstep. All his clothes were dropped into a bath of Jeyes fluid or Lysol, and he had to wash himself down with this disinfectant before she would let him in the house.

He spent most of his precious leave combing my hair with a small-toothed comb, because I'd been at school for six months – and I'd got nits. In those days, they didn't have the chemicals that they have now. I had long, fair hair – not very long, but enough to make it quite a job.

I was very lucky in my parents. They were both good-tempered, calm people – which is more than I can say about my grandparents!

We had moved back to Smokey House for a time in 1917. I remember it was a very fierce winter, and soon after Christmas. I had been given a china doll in a soldier's khaki uniform. It had been snowing, and the house was terribly cold because there had been no fires in it. I remember seeing my doll lying in a box in the attic (because I really wasn't very interested in dolls), and seeing apples spread out on the attic floor.

We then went back to the Hall for a while.

When old Kenneth came back from the war – seeing that his son wasn't interested in shooting – he sold the estate in 1919, and they moved nearer to London. But we were at the Hall until I was almost five, which brought us nearly to the end of the war – 1918.

Phyllis aged three   *Phyllis aged five*

Christmas in the trenches 1917

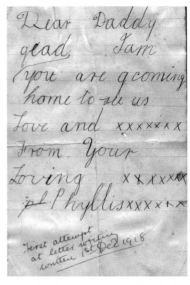

Phyllis' first letter to her father written from the Hall

The Signal Corps took a lithographic printer to war with them and made their own menus and Christmas cards despite their grim circumstances

Chapter Four

"I was lucky in my parents"

LIFE AT GORLESTON

When my father came home after the war, in September 1919, it was thought he would be for an early death.

We moved back to Gorleston, and rented quite a large house at 8, Beccles Road, with a long back garden that ran down to the allotments. It was the sort of house where, undoubtedly, at one time there had been a maid.

He was in a very nervous state. He never talked much about the war, but he had had a bad time. I know he had been gassed, and that he had been running a front-line telephone exchange, putting it up in advance of the troops, with mules for transport. Later, he had been in the Army of Occupation, in Köln.

By the time he came back, he had heart trouble and terrible boils. He was a very sick man. It was obvious there was no question of any more children, and he was off work for a year. Father should, I suppose, have had some sort of war pension but – like a lot of people – he refused to go before an Army Medical Board to be examined.

Post office pay wasn't very good – let alone sick pay.

They had put up a lovely wallpaper in my room, with nursery rhymes on it, which was then quite rare – 'Hickety, pickety, my black hen'...'Jack and Jill'. I loved my little room over the front hall. But we were very hard up. Mother did everything she could to help. She grew lettuces and cabbages, and took on two allotments. She kept chickens, and sold the eggs. In 1919, eggs were quite a good price, though the price collapsed quite swiftly afterwards.

Father eventually went back to work at Yarmouth Post Office, but he was frequently ill and never well enough to do all the extra work needed if you were going to progress in the Post Office.

At Gorleston, there were trams but virtually no cars. There were bathing machines on the beach. Bathing costumes still came down below the knee and below the elbow. They were high around the neck... and preferably black!

Mother and I started going to morning service at Gorleston Parish Church. We had a man who read the Bible marvellously, Ben Peart. He was a Gorleston man with a slight Norfolk accent. He wasn't an academic, but he read the Bible as it was meant to be read – a wonderful voice, and in that glorious prose of the 16th/17th century.

Mother also took in lodgers... insisting only that, on Sundays, they would have a cold supper so she could go to evening service.

I was six and a bit, and started at the Edward Worlledge School, Yarmouth, where I was stuck at the back of the second infants' room and allowed to 'get on with it' because I could already read, write and do arithmetic. Most of the others couldn't read. There were 60-odd children in the class. Well, after a month or so, Mother asked me to read a recipe one day, while she was cooking. And I couldn't. I'd forgotten how to read. Mother must have gone down to that school in a raging temper, because

I was promptly moved into the next class, where they all read every day.

And one had to be very neat. There was writing practice for at least a quarter of an hour every afternoon. I was made to take a copybook home, and do pages and pages of hooks.

It's no use teaching children to read unless you keep them in practice.

Mother was a very friendly, outgoing woman – kind but at the same time, like me, she would stick up for herself. She wouldn't be trodden under. Very direct.

Mother once grew some lettuces, and she'd got more than she needed so she took them up to the little vegetable shop in the high road. The woman was selling lettuces at two pence each, but she only offered Mother a halfpenny. Mother said she wanted a penny. When the woman refused, she stood outside the shop and gave them away. That was Mother.

As a child, living in Hampshire, she had had cataracts on both eyes when she was about six. She had spent 18 months in Moorfields Eye Hospital – a fortnight at a time, and a fortnight staying with her aunt in Walthamstow. Because of this long hospitalisation, mother only had the sight – so to speak – of one eye – and not very good sight at that.

Long illnesses do affect people. I'm sure if it hadn't been for that, Mother would have been a more... rampageous... character. As it was, she was very controlled, very quiet but firm. She was a good teacher, and devoted to teaching. But there were no outward signs of affection in our family. I don't think I was ever kissed goodnight and, in fact, I carried on in the same way. I'm very fond of children, but I didn't really kiss my own children goodnight.

However, I was lucky in my parents. My father ought to have been a teacher. It's a shame he wasn't. He was so marvellous with children, and could teach them anything. He was a very placid man. I don't think I ever heard my parents shout at each other, or have an acrimonious argument. They didn't see eye-to-eye over politics, always, but there was never any ill feeling. They both loved gardening and sailing, and they both cycled.

Every year, they would take their three weeks' holiday in June, sailing on the Broads and camping.

When he first came back, in 1919, my father had bought an old shrimp boat, with high gunwales, a great high stern and a great thick mast. The mast was laid out along the hall in Beccles Road and everybody – including me, at seven – was given a spokeshave to shave the mast down to a reasonable size!

He had taken the gunwales down, taken the stern down, had the tabernacle altered. Eventually, we used to go down on summer Sundays and sail. You could get as far as Burgh Castle and perhaps Reedham if the tide was right, coming back in the evening. Father had a boatshed on Cobholm Island.

Most of the Post Office staff were sorting clerks (SCs), but Father was a sorting/telegraphy clerk (STC) – which meant he could tap out the Morse Code. So he ran the special post office on the fish wharf during the fishing season, which meant a lot of hard work. He had a telegraph boy, and there were always a lot of telegrams which were put out with a Morse tapper. He perhaps had to account for £3,000 a day from the fish buyers and sellers. Apparently, there was no bank – so the post office acted as bank as well.

He had to be there at eight in the morning, and I don't think they shut until six at night at that time.

My mother was one of the first people to have electricity in the Yarmouth area. It was being popularised in the early 1920s and you could get some of your electrical work done for nothing – as an advertisement for electricity. So mother plunged in, and got lighting and – indeed – an electric stove.

The cellar had room for an incubator, so in early Spring each year we hatched all our own chicks. We kept the brooder for the young chicks in the middle kitchen. The place always smelled of paraffin in Spring. Sometimes Mother would wake up with a start and say "Jack, I can smell paraffin. I think the brooder's smoking." He'd have to get up and check, otherwise the little chicks would come out black in the morning!"

She worked very hard. They both did.

She also kept pure-bred chickens, exhibiting them in poultry shows, and won prizes – which meant that she could sell a setting of eggs from her pure-bred hens for as much as £3, which was as much as a lot of people were earning in a week. I remember how we used to oil their feet and combs and wattles before a show, and smooth down their feathers. Oh, they were gorgeous creatures – Wyandottes, Anconas and Suffolks.

Of course, our main layers were mongrels.

After the harvest, we used to go gleaning for corn around Burgh Castle and Belton. We always went gleaning, right from when I was a small child.

On another occasion, when they had looked at a house on the Lowestoft Road with a view to buying it (though I don't know what with), she'd had to give £5 key money to the estate agent to look at it. £5 was probably as much as my father earned in a week, so she was determined to get the money back. Every time she saw the estate agent in the street – in his top hat and long frock coat, pin-striped trousers – talking to his friends, she would ask for her £5. Every week, she also called at his house, and asked the housekeeper for the money.

I think it took her 10 months or a year. Eventually, one week, when she called, the housekeeper arrived with the £5 in her hand and said: There you are? and don't come again. It took a lot of spunk for her to get back £5!

People were very poor in the early 1920s. There was a family at the back of us with a smallholding. They used to get the herrings that were brought round by the boys off the drifters – and you could get an awful lot of fresh herrings on a string for six pence. They would salt their herrings in tubs, and that would be their staple food for the winter – plus potatoes they had grown and apples from the trees in their garden.

A lot of people lived like that. But we were always well fed.

I went to Good's Dance Hall, to learn to dance. The floor was so slippery that it looked like glass. I shall never forget the feeling of having to cross this enormous floor like an ice rink, terrified of falling down. But it was fun. You did a lot of marching to music, coming down in twos and splitting up, coming down in fours, eights, perhaps 16s... then reducing again. We were taught the Boston Two-step, the waltz and the foxtrot... at seven years old!

It had been decided that, having had two years of music lessons at Sudbourne, I'd better be taught the piano properly. A little way from our house was a Dame School – with perhaps 10 or 12 pupils in a long room at the back of the house, run by Old Mrs Bensley and her daughter, Miss Hilda Bensley.

It was an old house, since pulled down, next to Gorleston Post Office. The place was full of cats, and stank. I used to take a deep breath before I went in, and make it last as long as possible.

Old Mrs Bensley was – to me at six years old – very, very old with terrible red-rimmed eyes. I couldn't bear to look at her. She was a little woman with a black frock nearly down to the floor, and her hair piled on top.

I wonder now if it was a wig...

Miss Hilda Bensley was nice, and she taught the piano. She had lots of letters after her name (LRAM). However, she was dubious when Mother first took me, and said she was full up.

Mother had brought some of my music along, and asked if she would just listen to me. So I was allowed to sit down at one of those old pianos with a fretwork front and two brass candlesticks. When Miss Bensley heard me, and found I could already read simple music, she decided that – yes – she could take me.

She was a brilliant pianist. Every year, she arranged a concert for the school at which she gave a demonstration. It was she who inculcated my love of Beethoven. She played all the sonatas.

She also had some wonderful boys' annuals and, since I was always early for my lesson and she always over-ran her time, I had a chance to read them... about the founding of the Boy Scouts, and how Baden-Powell could write with his right hand and draw a picture with his left simultaneously. That stayed in my memory for a long while.

Well, then I had one lesson a week there for years – and I took my first exam when I was seven at the town hall in Yarmouth – which I passed with credit. Nervous? No! I was so confident! I knew I could do it. Of course, that attitude did not last. Every year I took an exam at the town hall, and there came a time when I wasn't so sure of myself. However, it was always exciting – rather nerve-racking later on, but it meant a day off school!

Mother was strict. She wouldn't have me yowling like a spoiled child, wanting this and that... And she was strict over my practising. So I got a penny an hour for piano practice. I had a money box. It was iron, and you could undo the screw at the bottom. I understood it was the tower of Köln Cathedral.

Father must have brought it back from Germany. I had to get up early. From seven till eight most mornings, I had piano practice. Then I got my penny. And what I didn't finish in the morning, I finished at night after school.

At school, I remember St George's Days, when Sgt Major Bolton would arrive in his uniform, a very short man. We had all this marching in the playground in twos, fours and eights. We sang '*God Save the King*' and '*Land of Hope and Glory*' – then had a half-holiday.

I seemed to go through the junior school like a dose of medicine. I don't remember being in any one class for more than a few months. By 10, I was in the senior school, the youngest there. The rest of the class were 11 or 12.

I was quite small at that age, but the second morning – when we lined up for assembly – the teacher who usually played the piano for hymns was away. Old Joe May, the headmaster, looked at the whole school spread out along the hall – 300 or 400 children – and said: "Can anybody play the hymn?"

There was a dead silence. So presently, I moved out and said: "I'll do it." Well, it was my job after that. Sight-reading didn't scare me, you see. I'd been used to my grandfather making me do it. It was second nature.

And my father played the banjo – not only by ear but from music. We had very happy evenings at Beccles Road playing hymns from the Salvation Army hymn book – "*Pull for the Shore, Sailor*" among others. We had a big book called '*Plantation Songs*'. We used to play quite a lot, he and I, in the winter months when it was dark, after I had done my homework.

He had a good ear and, if I was playing something, he could pick it up. We would play for an hour or so at a time... and sing. Mother enjoyed it. Later, we played jazz together.

Mother had played the violin when she was young, but I never heard her play. Her mother played the concertina.

We had a strong religious education at the Edward Worlledge. There was always a reading and a hymn at assembly. Miss Brunning taught scripture, in a room of 60 children with platforms going up. I can see her standing there. She was tall and dark, with a beautiful voice. I still remember a lot of the Bible that we had to learn by heart, one piece each week. I particularly remember the 13th chapter of Corinthians. She insisted that we did it over and over and over again... until we understood what we were reading:

"Though I speak with the tongues of men and of angels, and have not charity, I am become as sounding brass, or a tinkling cymbal..."

We had French – very peculiar French – with Miss James. She was reputed to be half-Spanish and half-Welsh, and she taught us phonetically. With 60 children, it wasn't easy but she would get very excited, and shout a lot. It might have been called frenetic French.

Miss Hunt – Polly Hunt – was short, dumpy... and very strict. The wickedest thing you could do in her class was eat a sweet. The heavens fell on you if you had an aniseed ball in your mouth so, of course, if you were really daring, you had a gobstopper... and showed your neighbour how it was changing colour every time you took it out of your mouth. But she certainly taught us: grammar, arithmetic, long division and multiplication. I think I was even taught percentages. I know that when I went to high school, I was well in advance of the arithmetic there.

Phyllis aged eight.
She recalled that the dress was green velvet with gold braid.

Smokey House Sudbourne circa 1890

*Ada and Great Grandma
Land at Smokey House*

Chapter Five

"It was a busy life"

SMOKEY HOUSE

All my holidays, the moment we broke up, very often the same day (because we used to break up at dinner time or 3pm in those days), I was put on the train to Wickham Market, to be picked up in the horse and cart and brought by my Grandfather Land to Smokey House.

Smokey House was thatched, and very old. It is marked on the John Norden 1606 map of the area, and had that name even then.

I can see me now, creeping down to see if Grandma and Grandpa were awake when the dawn chorus was on, and woke me in the summer – because I slept in the attic, and I'd hear this wonderful noise from all the birds in the wood. It was so loud! All the different birds would be singing and chirping – cocks crowing and cuckoos. And I hadn't got a clock, so I'd creep down (because it wouldn't do to wake them). It must have been about 4 o'clock, with the sun just getting up in the east.

If they were still asleep, I had to go back to bed again and read. Then I'd hear them stirring, round about five o'clock. Breakfast at six – thick slices of home-cured ham and eggs.

Remembering the tremendously thick walls, I suppose it was probably a clay lump/wattle and daub house, bricked on the outside at a later date. Originally, it would have had just a ladder inside – or rather, two ladders because it was a three-storey house with rooms in the attic.

Stairs had been put in by this time, up beside an enormous chimney, which warmed the cupboards in our upstairs bedrooms, used for airing clothes. They were always warm. So if you were really cold... you could go and stand in the cupboard!

The bedrooms faced east, and we kept a pair of binoculars on the window sill to look out for boats on the sea, or watch aircraft as they practised dropping bombs over Halvergate Island. Through binoculars, you could see them quite clearly as they leaned out and dropped the bombs by hand.

We had paraffin lamps. That meant that one read in the daylight. In the evenings, one played cards. So I was taught at a very early age: brag, whist, halfpenny nap, crib. We also played 'High, Low, Jack and the Game', which was more complicated than crib. So from the time I was about three, I could count up to 31 – for crib.

We played for nuts except at Christmas, when we played for money. So I had a very intensive education.

By the time I was seven, Grandfather had taught me not only how to play whist – but to remember every card, who played it, and how to draw the inference of what they'd got left. ("Ask yourself WHY did he play that card.")

So one evening, we walked down to Orford Town Hall...

It was quite a big whist drive. Can you imagine the horror with which these old men – you know, the ones who really thought they could play – viewed this child walking in (already way past her bedtime), and being brought to the table as their partner!

But I could deal and cut as well as any of them, and I had the most amazing luck that night. I got the grand slam twice with my partner, and won first prize!

Mother was very strict about bedtimes, but I can remember – when my mother wasn't there – being put to bed at half-past six, then being brought down again at eight to play whist because they needed me to make up a foursome!

After dinner, they always had 20 minutes' nap, and even as a small child I had to be quiet. I always sat in this wicker chair, knitting. I had been taught at an early age, and by the time I was seven or eight, my holiday job would be re-footing Grandad's stockings. (He wore breeches, not trousers.)

It was a very busy life. I always had to do my chores before I was allowed out with my grandfather, and what a lot of work there was. There was always something: I could wash up, wipe up, put away... shell the peas, peel the potatoes.

With no electricity, everything had to be done by hand. All the rooms had carpets except the kitchen. After they'd been brushed, the job of any young person – ie me – was to go over and pick up any bits that were stuck to the carpet. It might take half an hour.

My grandfathers were, I think, disappointed that they did not have a boy. I was the only grandchild, so undoubtedly I was always brought up to do things they would have been teaching their grandsons... forking, or helping with the haystack, mucking out a stable etc.

I think this, later, rather shocked Ted... who rather thought girls should be brought up to sew a fine seam and not, if necessary, to handle a gun!

The house stood by itself, in a couple of acres of ground. A birch wood behind us was more than two fields away from the village and our nearest neighbours. But I don't think we ever missed going to church on a Sunday, walking down.

My grandfather put hurdles across the yard to stop dogs – and me – getting out, and also to stop tramps getting in. There were a lot of tramps at the end of the war. Many of them had been in the Army and couldn't find a job afterwards. So they just trudged from workhouse to workhouse – which were set a day's walk apart. There was one at Snape, one at Hales, another near Saxmundham, and workhouses on the way to Woodbridge and Ipswich.

The men would be kept in until about 10am, then sent out with a lump of bread and cheese. They had to go to the next workhouse, and we were on the route.

The tramps would come to the hurdle and say: "Could I have some hot water?" – which meant, of course, that you'd give them a pot of tea. At dinner time, you gave them a plate of food. Then after they'd gone, you looked around to see if they'd left a mark on your fence. Most of them carried a bit of chalk, and a chalked sign on your fence might mean: "This is a good place to call" or "Fierce dogs here" or "These people will give you anything you ask for" or "No dogs here". You never quite knew what the marks meant, so you looked around, and made sure you rubbed them off.

It was a hard time.

It was a hard life for the keepers, too. Undoubtedly, they used to have their whack of pheasants, rabbits and hares when nobody was looking. But they weren't paid very much. One of the things I was taught very early on was to answer any inquisitive questions with "I don't know". ("What did you have for dinner today?" "I don't know.") Because there were always people – not so much the other keepers or servants at the Hall, but people in the village – who were ready to catch you out.

So it was drilled into you that if anybody asked questions, you should say: "Ask Grandma" or "I don't know". It made you out a bit daft, I suppose. Or you would say "We had chicken". That was alright. Or a rabbit. But you did NOT say you'd had pheasant...or a hare...or a duck!

I have often thought that, of the two, my grandmother was the really strong character. She was outgoing, friendly and generous, and didn't mind what she did for people but – like my own mother – right was right, and wrong was wrong. No nonsense. Both my grandmothers were excellent needlewomen, and made all their husbands' clothes. Grandma even made his keeper's hats – you know, tied on the top with a bow.

In winter, over his long, hand-knitted stockings, he would have leather buskins that fitted over his boots and breeches.

In the summer, he'd have soft leather gaiters unless it was very wet. No Wellington boots in those days, but your winter boots would be always dubbined thoroughly, so they were more or less waterproof.

All the clothes for the keepers were made by the local tailor. Grandfather had two suits a year because he didn't wear the keepers' tough corduroy twill suits; he had a sort of heather tweed, which was also hard-wearing and thorn-proof.

Keepers had one suit a year, and two pairs of boots and gaiters. They were given all the coal they wanted, all the wood they liked to collect. The coal came in a railway truck from Wickham Market. They used to take the truck off the rails, with horses, and share the coal out among the keepers.

And boots – again, he was given two pairs a year. They must have worn out very quickly. They were all hand-made on lasts over at Benhall.

When I started doing the books, Grandad – as head keeper – got something like 35 old shillings a week. But there were no rates, and insurance on the house was paid by the boss. He had all the horse's food free and – I think – all the paraffin he needed.

Then when there was a big shoot – perhaps 30 people – and it was up to Grandad to hire beaters and so on, there used to be marvellous tips. And not only tips – but you'd get financial wizards coming down and giving you ideas about how to invest your money – saying, you know: "You want to buy so-and-so shares this week". So Grandad was very well off.

They used to have some marvellous shooting parties. Edward VII, Queen Victoria's son, used to come there – the one who bought Sandringham. So did George V.

It must have once been a quite extensive farm. Grandma's kitchen was huge, and at one end, you went down three deep brick steps into what was called the 'cellar' – but had obviously once been a dairy, and which was even older than the house. It was half below ground, with marble shelves. In winter, a stream ran right across the cellar floor. It was always very cold.

The kitchen had a big Bath stone sink which drained across the yard and – eventually – into a not-particularly-salubrious pond. I think the stables also drained into it.

There were sides of bacon hanging in the kitchen and two coppers – one for beer, the other – next to the cooking range – for washing clothes. Once, for about a year, a tame squirrel lived over the top of the clothes copper on an arrangement of branches.

Brewing beer was a five-day job. Grandma used to make three 'nines'. First came nine gallons of strong beer. You'd put probably 12 gallons of water into the copper to start with, along with hops and malt, bring it to the boil and add some sugar and liquorice. That would go in one cask and be worked.

Then she'd make nine gallons of medium on the next brew by adding more water to the ingredients, and finally nine gallons of what she called 'washings', which was very thin beer suitable for children. I remember drinking it from a very early age – probably not terribly alcoholic.

So there were always three nine-gallon casks in the cellar waiting to be tapped. It was a splendid cellar, always chickens hung up, ready to be plucked and – in season – cold boiled asparagus and cold boiled broad beans for our suppers.

There were a couple of acres of land around the house.

Outside the back door was a big, grassy yard with a coal shed, a game larder and – at the side – a pump, with a trough that could be filled up so the animals could drink. There was an enormous L-shaped barn, with room for two carts – a 'governess' cart and a dogcart – plus a workbench where Grandad made his rabbit snares. It also held stalls which could accommodate two or three visiting horses.

At the back, the barn led into our own stable for two horses – though we only had one – and a tack room.

There was a partially-walled garden, where we raised pheasant chicks, and a cookhouse where the oats, dog biscuits and chicken meal were kept in metal bins with heavy lids. This room also had a big stone sink and a fire. The fire always had a pot on with little potatoes in it. I used to eat the little potatoes, unscrubbed though they were, when they were emptied out into the sink, ready to be mixed with the chickens' food. They were delicious.

In the yard, there was always a bracken stack – because the horses were littered down with dried bracken – and an enormous muckheap with horse manure and – of course – pails from the house. The manure heap was always kept in extremely good order, built properly, so that you had old manure ready for the gardens at the front, and the new manure heap at the back – where the smell was not so offensive.

Sudbourne village was very poor. My grandmother used to pay one of the village women, Mrs Goldsmith, to come on a Wednesday and do the washing by hand, peg it out, scrub the enormous kitchen floor and various other jobs. She'd be given 'elevens' – home-brewed beer or cocoa –

and a good meal at dinnertime, but it was a long day's work for half a crown. Mrs Goldsmith had a consumptive husband who couldn't work.

There was a large wicket gate – taller than I was, and always painted red for some reason – which shut off the house yard from the chickens' yard. Then there was a long chicken house, where chickens and turkeys lived, something like 100 or 200 at a time. Attached, but shut off by a heavy door, was a game room where they hung pheasants, rabbits, partridges, duck and hares ready to be packed into baskets and go up to the London market at Smithfield.

There was an octagonal building, which must once have been a summerhouse, with a saw-horse, where all the wood was stacked ready for winter. Big logs were cut up outside with a two-handed cross-cut saw, then put under cover so the man could work inside if it was raining.

In the corner of the house yard, next to the chickens' yard, was a two-seater lavatory (one tall one for grown-ups and a small one for children) surrounded by tall fir trees and a privet hedge. At night, you went down with a candle, and hoped it didn't blow out before you got there! We also had a torch – a joke torch. When you turned it on, a canvas-covered snake jumped out of the end. That was great fun to give to visitors.

The whole estate was very feudal. It was 30,000 acres, with various lodges scattered around. Originally there had been 30 keepers, but younger men had gone to the war and few remained. Grandfather had been beyond calling-up age.

We'd got Edmund Caley down near Iken, Kersey in the Reydon area... There was Chillesford Lodge, which was south-west. Then, the other side of us, half a mile up the road, The White Lodge where another keeper, England, lived. Then there was The Villa , which was the east lodge, where the estate secretary lived – a rather posher house.

The lodges were – what shall I say? – imitation Tudor, and extremely inconvenient, all frightfully antique on the outside, with bits of wood stuck on but, on the inside, tiny rooms and a damp, dark kitchen. Looking back, keepers' wives didn't have much of a life. Most of the keepers lived right out in the middle of nowhere. Kersey didn't even have a proper road to his house.

There was The Nursery, half a mile from us, where plants were grown ready for the gardens at the Hall. Then there was The Black Lodge, which must have been the west lodge, where Georgie Welham lived with his ancient wife. 'Old Georgie' he was called... and if he wasn't old, he damned well looked it! I always thought he was about 80, but he was referred to as our 'boy'.

It was reputed that Old Georgie, in his younger days on some occasion of national celebration, had climbed to the top of Orford Castle and stood on his head. To me, as a child, this was incredible. The things one remembers!

Old Georgie, for the few years that I remember him before he retired, was a very bad-tempered old man. His job was to look after the chickens and turkeys. And the horse. Saw all the wood. Do the gardening. Cut all the hedges. Go and do the beating for shooting parties. Help with the pheasants when we were rearing them. Then he had to pump all the water and bring it indoors, fill the coppers. In fact, his job was to do anything he was asked... perhaps it's no wonder Old Georgie was bad-tempered!

Grandma looked after the front garden, which had two little patches of grass and flower borders, but we also had two big vegetable gardens – one each side of the house – with asparagus beds, rhubarb beds, and all sorts of fruit trees including great big Victoria plums. There were also currant bushes, raspberries and strawberries.

At the west end of Grandma's garden, between the back door and the pantry, was an enormous table, so huge that it must have been built there; it would have taken about eight men to lift it, and it was covered with all the boots and shoes of the family. All Grandad's winter boots were dubbined, all his summer boots highly polished.

That was another of Old Georgie's jobs every day – to collect the dirty boots and shoes, clean them and – when they were scrupulously clean – assemble them on this table, ready to be put on.

I don't think he got more than £1 a week plus his house, but he got a good dinner.

Grandma cooked a big midday meal every day, and Old Georgie had an enormous plateful. He didn't eat it in the house with us. He ate in the cookhouse, where they cooked the chickens' food. Old Georgie seemed to eat so much that I sometimes wonder if he took some home in a bag for his wife. I shouldn't wonder.

It was a hard life for an old man. I think he retired when Lloyd George brought in the first pension – 10 shillings then, from the age of 70. Old Georgie was then replaced by 'Young Nash', who had just left school and was the son of one of the keepers.

Perhaps surprisingly, we had a telephone system – a sort of board with various holes that you put a peg into, then wound a handle furiously to make it ring at the other end. There was a hole to connect you to the Hall, and one for each of the keepers' lodges. We could also be connected to the Post Office at Orford.

Of course, the telephone exchange at Orford was a very simple affair. It was more or less a table with, again, holes in it and pegs for everyone who had a telephone.

There weren't many people you could ring up in any case and, of course, the woman who looked after it at the Post Office got all the news, because she would listen in to everything that was said. It was well-known that the Misses Voyle – there were two of them – listened in, and passed the news on to everyone if it was interesting!

Eliza and Edwin Land at Smokey House

Great-grandfather William Land

Great-grandmother Mary Land

Grandmother Eliza Land

Grandfather Edwin Land

Edward Chambers, Lucy Rebecca Debenham and
Edwin Land circa 1880 possibly at Southampton

Chapter Six

"It was a lovely time to live"

KEEPERING

There was always an enormous sack of rice in the pantry to feed the dogs on – probably about 2cwt – because Grandad used to breed and break Labradors and retrievers, and train them as gundogs as a sideline.

We had a row of kennels, brick-built at the bottom and topped with tall iron spikes, concrete floors with wooden bunks that probably had hay on them, and a drinking trough in the corner. There were central heating pipes running through them for the dogs. No central heating in the house, I might add!

Two of the kennels were double, so that when there were puppies there was more room for the mother.

A large saucepan – like an iron fish kettle – would be put on the kitchen range. Rabbits would be roughly skinned and chopped, and put in the pot – bones and all – with water. The skins, if they were good, were always pinned out, ready for the man who came round to buy them for about a penny each. Moleskins were also pegged out on the big barn doors.

There was no business about you taking the bones out of the dogs' food. They had been brought up to it, so they didn't 'wolf' their food down so fast they might choke. Our dogs ate everything they were given – including one who loved raw onions!

So when the rabbits were half cooked, the rice would be poured in, and that would be the dogs' evening meal.

In the morning, they would each have one of the big Spratts Victoria biscuits. I think that was their complete diet.

They were always in excellent order. They never got fat, as retrievers do when they are fed as pets, and they weren't castrated because they were sold on as breeding dogs. So whenever you took them out, you could always feel proud that they were in such fine fettle, so full of life. It was a lovely time to live.

Very often, at the end of the season, you'd get these dogs back that you'd already trained because they'd been spoiled, given titbits under the table and not made to keep to heel. They'd got fat and lazy and disobedient. So they would come for retraining.

When a dog came back, and had been thoroughly spoiled, he would be shut in the kennels with plenty of water and a Spratts biscuit. Perhaps for three or four days he wouldn't touch the biscuit. When he was sufficiently hungry, and ate the biscuit, then his retraining could begin. Then he'd be fed on rice and rabbits.

I've no doubt Grandad was paid well, because there weren't many people training dogs, and we had dogs in the kennels most of the time.

In spring, we'd go to Wickham Market, Saxmundham market and other markets round about with a dogcart, and buy up broody (or 'setty') hens cheaply at perhaps 6d or a shilling each, or get them from local villagers. Then we would have something like 3000 pheasants' eggs sent up in large wickerwork hampers, all packed in straw. They all had to be carefully unpacked, then kept in wooden egg racks and turned once a week, if not more often.

Wire netting pens for the hens were put out in the walled part of the garden. You had a row of coops that each took perhaps eight hens, each hen separated with her own run.

We'd been careful to get rid of the rats first. Rat poisoning always went on during January and February. You put down oats and sugar for three days, and then the fourth day you put strychnine down – carefully, under tiles. Then you picked up the dead rats.

Then you put each hen in her own place, and put a china egg under them. If they came off being broody, that was alright – you put them in with the laying chickens. But once a hen had shown her mettle, and was remaining broody, at the end of a week or so, then you could put down 15 or 20 pheasants' eggs under her. So, with 3000 eggs, we needed a lot of hens!

During the sitting season, which lasted about three weeks, it was all hands on deck. Every morning, you had to go out and raise and peg the middle section of the coop to give all the hens their 20 minutes off, let them get a little exercise in their runs, and fluff up their feathers. They were turned off the nest, fed – usually with soaked maize – and watered. Then they went back, after we had made sure none of the eggs were cracked or broken.

Then, of course, once they were hatched out it was full-time work. When the pheasant chicks were old enough, and grew stronger, they would be taken to various stands around the estate where there was a keepers' hut.

The hens and their coops would be put up there with the little chicks to start with. So then the hen would cluck to the pheasants, and by this time they knew what a hen's cluck meant.

If strangers went up or animals were about, you'd see the chicks getting in among the feathers or sometimes sitting on the backs of the hens with their heads poking out.

The keepers would be on duty with them night and day, two at a time, right through the season. At first, they would catch and kill rabbits, boil them on a little fire, take the meat off the bone and chop it up. Hens' eggs had to be hard-boiled and chopped up fine.

That was the first pheasants' food. Gradually, they would be introduced to split corn and other food. Once the young poults were bigger, the hens were taken back to join the throng in the chicken house, and the feeding of the young poults was reduced.

My grandfather had a shepherd's hut up in the birch wood, where he kept sacks of corn. And the pheasants were fed up there, night and morning. The corn was spread out, over possibly a couple of acres of the birch wood. He had a chemical which smelled a bit like aniseed, which you rubbed on your hands, and then rubbed on the corn. The pheasants couldn't resist it – so it was guaranteed to keep them at home, and stop them wandering too far before the shooting started in the winter.

It was an interesting life. After my chores were done, my grandfather often took me out in the dogcart as he made his calls. We went all over the estate.

The Tunstall Walks were lovely, all gorse down one side and plovers nesting in the spaces. In those days, one was allowed to pick up plovers' eggs and boil and eat them. The other side of the road was all thyme and heather. I can almost smell it now – absolutely gorgeous! Now it has been planted with fir trees from Tunstall right down to Iken, practically.

We walked there a lot. Grandad caught a lot of his rabbits there, using snares he made himself, out in the big barn, from four strands of thin copper wire twisted into a loop and pegs. There were thousands of rabbits then.

We didn't use spring-traps a lot, except to catch rats.

He had a little dog called 'Whiskey'. She was 17 when she died, and I suppose I was five then. And all the family – everyone – sat around and cried, including Grandfather. I'd never seen a man cry before. She used to come with us in the dogcart and she'd run along ahead of the horse , even when she was getting old. When she was tired, she'd sit down in the middle of the road, and the horse would stop. Then we would have to get down and pick her up.

We went round the marshes, down to Butley and Iken. Sometimes we went to the mill at Chillesford Lodge, to get meal and stuff for the chickens. That was a most interesting place... Watching all these belts and wheels whizzing round when they were grinding. And very dusty. You could hardly see across the room when they were working, and you came out practically covered! It wasn't a windmill, or even a very posh mill. It was powered by an old engine. But to me it was very exciting.

I think I was very lucky, being able to have that sort of life when I was a child. I wasn't learning natural history, exactly. Grandma knew her plants. But with Grandad, it was keepering – country life.

On a Sunday afternoon we went round the farms – all of which were let by the estate. The farmers had certain duties. They had to keep their gateways in repair, for example, otherwise there would be a fuss by the agent. One of Grandad's duties was to keep an eye open, on his visits to the farms, to see if anything needed doing. Or if some farmer had a complaint about something, Grandad might say a good word for him.

But sometimes the journey, for me, meant 'home time'. Then there'd be all the trauma of getting to the station, seeing the train come in and thinking the holiday was over, and I'd got to go back to school and live in Gorleston again.

It took an hour and a half to get to Wickham Market if we didn't hurry – seven and a half miles. If it was raining, we had an American rug to put over us, a black mackintosh rug with plaid lining that fastened on two hooks so that you were completely covered up to the waist ... and, hopefully, you'd all got your mackintoshes and hats with you!

Up until the 1920s, there was very little communication between the villages. Most villages had their own corn mill, they killed their own meat, had their own butchers, blacksmith etc. They had fishing, they could bab for eels. They were self-sufficient, and I don't think people today realise how restricted travel was.

Russell, by the time he was 16, had never been out of Surlingham. He told me: "I had to go to Bramerton when I was 16 with a message for my mother. She wound a scarf around my neck and told me to be careful – because it was three miles."

There was a weekly horse and cart to Woodbridge, to the market. It was in 1920 that this cart was replaced by a 'motey-car', as it was called – a van. So rather more people could travel then. But you still probably had someone's pig in the van with you. Although wages were still very low, there was a little more spare money about, and you had some cheap shops setting up in Woodbridge.

Around 1920, an ex-soldier started coming round in a van, and he would buy eggs off Grandma for a shilling for 20 – which was quite a good price – and she could buy elastic, bits of ribbon, lace and writing paper.

I remember, in 1917, before my aunt's wedding, the dressmaker had come out from Woodbridge, and stayed for three or four days. She made the wedding dress, the bridesmaids' dresses – I was a bridesmaid – and grandmother's dress, underwear, petticoats, nightdresses... all in three days, working 12 hours a day on Grandmother's Jones Treadle Sewing Machine. Then she had to be taken back to Woodbridge on the dogcart – 10 miles.

1919 was a year of great change. Seeing that his son was not interested in shooting, that was the year Mr Clark sold Sudbourne Hall to Walter Boynton and moved closer to London. He would, in turn, sell it to Lord Manton, and Grandfather stayed on through these changes.

Grandma still played her round of golf on the nine-hole course, winter and summer. Grandad stayed there until he retired. Neither of my grandfathers wanted to move. They were happy in their work, and that was that. So Grandfather Land was well over 70 when he eventually retired from Sudbourne Hall.

Lord Manton was an extraordinarily nice man, who really cared about people. He was behind Watson's Matchless Cleanser – a soap – and had marvellous plans for the villagers. He was going to have proper windows and bathrooms put in the cottages.

He had new servants' quarters built – which are still standing. Most of the Hall has been pulled down, apart from the stable yard. The building looked a bit like a hospital. It was rather ugly and out of keeping, but very comfortable inside with all mod cons including electricity.

He unfortunately died in 1922 in a riding accident. The horse stuck its hoof in a rabbit hole and threw him. Then the estate was split between his sons. One son, Alistair Watson, took Chillesford Lodge and tried various businesses including growing blackcurrants and redcurrants, making a warren to breed rabbits and laying out a polo ground.

My grandfather still stayed for a time, but I think he found things were getting rather difficult. He retired in 1929. I was 16.

It was heart-breaking, leaving Sudbourne Hall. They had been there for 30 years. My grandparents moved to Yardley Hastings, to a rather horrible house built on a hill – so that the sitting room window was actually 12 feet above the road but you had to go down five steps to get in the back door. That was how my grandmother eventually died. She was 86, and she'd climbed up the steps to clean the outside front window, and fell. She died three months later, in 1938 – the year I was married.

Grandad had died a year earlier – in (I think) August 1937. He had broken his leg. They took him to hospital, but the leg wouldn't mend. He'd only been ill twice in his life: once when his gun exploded and he lost the sight of his right eye, the other when he'd been attacked by poachers in Hampshire and left for dead.

Sudbourne Hall was mainly destroyed during the Second World War, because all the people were evacuated and the Army moved in. The birch and heather woods at the back of Smokey House were used as a tank exercise ground. But I always call it 'home', you know. I still think of Sudbourne as home.

Edwin Land and his dog

*Phyllis in the sixth form at Yarmouth High School
(second from the left, back row)*

Phyllis, Evelyn and Ada at St Olaves 'bungalow'

Chapter Seven

"St Olave's... a place of butterflies and insects.."

HIGH SCHOOL YEARS

In the Spring of 1924, the British Empire Exhibition was on at Wembley. Children from school came back with horrifying tales of paper sheets to sleep on and paper cups to drink from. I went in July, staying with my aunt and uncle in London. I remember crowds and crowds of people, and magnificent Japanese and Italian displays... the first grapefruit I had ever tasted or even seen. I can't say I enjoyed it. I'd never tasted anything so sour in my life. They were not like grapefruits today.

That year, I went to Yarmouth High School. I sat the scholarship in February 1924 – (not everyone took the 11-plus in those days; we were a select few.) Then I had an interview with Miss Hague at the High School in June.

Mother bought me a new frock for the interview. I know we were very hard up. Post Office pay had been cut in the early 1920s. Wages were very low and, of course, things got gradually worse until the 1930s. The 1930s were dreadful, much worse than the early 1980s.

So my frock was bought in the sales. I can still see it now. It was what was called a Shepherd's Plaid, very close black squares on a cream background which gave the effect of being grey, with a blue trim. I thought I was very smart, but it was probably a rather terrible frock to go to an interview in. It was slightly too big. The sleeves and hem had to be turned up.

Anyway, I got into the B class. So I can't have done too badly. There were only a dozen of us scholarship girls that year, and I think we were regarded rather as oddities, but it was very exciting to go to a new school, and an all-girls' school – no boys, not so rough.

I was supposed to mend my own black stockings when I went to the High School but – because Mother's eyes weren't very good – I remember putting black lead on my legs underneath the hole when I hadn't mended them!

Yarmouth High School was in a lovely old house on the seafront, with a tower and a beautiful, elegant staircase. One COULDN'T really slouch down a staircase like that! It taught one to come down stairs decently (though there was also a back staircase that you could take two-at-a-time!)

There was a purpose-built science laboratory on the far side of the playground, and an annexe where younger girls, who were being paid for, were taught. I suppose, on the whole, they were eight, nine and 10. The High School was gradually getting larger at that time.

Soon I was playing the piano again.

We had a gym teacher who used to play for country dancing. She played so appallingly that one day I just went up to her, and said: "Wouldn't you like me to play the country dances for you, Miss Reardon?" I think she was quite grateful. It wasn't long before I was playing the hymns, as well. The girl who usually played at assembly had terrible chilblains in the winter... so bad that she had to play with gloves on. Once again, they were quite glad that somebody else could play.

That year I had my first bicycle, 30 shillings second-hand, done up like new – beautifully painted. It took all my Christmas and holiday money for about two years.

Father had been ill again, and the doctor said he ought to get out in the country.

So, since he was mad about sailing, he decided to get a wooden 20-by-10 hut, ex-Army stock, which was practically new and quite cheap, and convert it into a sort of riverside bungalow. He rented space on a farm at St Olave's on the marsh. They got the hut down there but, of course, to get to St Olave's one needed to cycle. It was six miles – quite a long ride on a small bicycle.

The very first time I went there, Mother and Father must have stopped to talk to the farmer, and I walked on ahead, and they arrived to find me covered in mud, just getting out of the dyke – having fallen off the plank bridge. Well, that was the first and last time. I never fell off a ligger after that!

We began to stay at St Olave's, and I would cycle to the Yarmouth High School on fine days, nearly 12 miles – wet days, I went on the train. The High School, then, was at the bottom of Trafalgar Road. But one was fairly tough, and St Olave's was great fun. I really enjoyed that.

Mother used to get as brown as a berry in the summer, and looked like a gypsy. She practically lived out of doors.

There wasn't the tourism then. You could sail for miles before you met a cruiser, and there were very few wherries left by the 1920s – perhaps 10. All the rivers were clean and sparkling. You could stop, put your tent up, and when you'd finished your food, lean over the side and wash your plates and cups in the river.

There were four of these 'bungaloids'. We were the last. There was a railway carriage which some teachers had, a tiny wooden bungalow occupied by a butcher and his family (I went to school with his children), and an old gypsy caravan on wheels.

Father partitioned our hut into a 10-by-10 living room, a bedroom for Father and Mother and a tiny, tiny bedroom for me. You could just about stand between the partition and the bed, and there was just room for a tiny chest of drawers under the window. He built bunks so that I could always have a friend to stay. He put a veranda on the front and a corrugated iron kitchen on the end, with a pail closet at the back. It was surprisingly comfortable.

The farm dog, Dandy, quickly attached himself to us – because when he'd had a bad paw, mother had wrapped it up and seen to it. There was a row of houseboats moored down the dyke which were also occupied at weekends. One belonged to Arthur Patterson (the writer and amateur naturalist). He was good company, and he'd always got something to talk about – the birds, fish, what was growing on the marshes. Later, he moved his houseboat down to Breydon but I always remember him being there when I was young.

Another houseboat belonged to Tommy Parker, a little lame man who was a tailor. His houseboat used to leak – so that every weekend when he came back the water was over the floor, and it had to be pumped out. Between them, he and Father and Arthur concocted a windmill from an old bicycle wheel with tin sails and chains connected to a little pump. This thing clattered around and pumped out the water. It did keep the boat fairly dry – but you can imagine the noise it made in a gale, rattling and banging and going round like one o'clock, nearly being torn out of its moorings!

St Olave's... a place of butterflies and insects, bracken on the hillside, wonderful flowers on the marshes, with a bridge across the dyke to an orchard behind the bungalow. There was a lane at the back of the farm, with crab apple trees and a cliff on one side.

We went there every weekend that we could. We all had bicycles, and I'd got friends who were only too pleased to come with me, particularly Evelyn Crannas (who always remained one of my firmest friends), Mary Appleby or Madge Lilly.

Every so often, we'd have a party of children up. They would come by train, and on bicycles. It was a great place for strawberry teas, parties in the summer and picnics. We really had a wonderful childhood out there, and it was all very simple – no wireless.

I remember fishing for eels and roach at the end of the dyke, and we used to swim across the river to the island and back. We used to dress up and do plays. Of course, once we went to St Olave's, church was out during the summer months. We still went in the winter.

At Gorleston, Evelyn and I would spend Saturdays together and – if Mother and Father went to the pictures – we'd sit in front of the fire and read ourselves silly, and perhaps not even speak a word to each other all the evening, just sit reading our library books.

Ted had joined the choir soon after his family came to Gorleston... a lovely treble voice he had, as a child. By 1924, he was 15. His voice had quite naturally gone down to tenor and, of course, he'd started cycling out to Belton and other places early on Sunday mornings. He usually used to arrive late at church – and come down the aisle with gumboots underneath his surplice!

In 1925, when I was 12, I was confirmed along with Evelyn and two or three other friends who went to school with me.

That year, Mother found she could let the whole house at Beccles Road to the bandmaster from Wellington Pier from May until September. So all our belongings were shut up in two big cupboards, and we went to the bungalow for the whole summer. It was great fun and, of course, it did pay the rates on the house... probably the rent, as well.

At the High School, Miss Haig was headmistress... very strict. I was in severe trouble because I was coming top of the class in exams, but bottom for work during the term. She made me stand up in assembly. There were about 360 girls there. Very embarrassing.

I wasn't one of the people who worked very hard, and I think my parents sort of let me get on with it, much as Ted and I did with our children. We didn't sit down with them and inspect their homework every night. Perhaps we should have done. I don't know if the children would have been any happier. You don't know, do you, when you are young? Bringing up children is largely experimental.

There was a Guides company associated with the High School, run by Miss Mary Taylor who taught maths. She was very clever and, once you learned your basic algebra and geometry, she was marvellous. But to start small children off, when they had no idea of 'x' and 'y' and Pythagoras... I'm afraid she was TOO clever. In my first year, I got terrible marks because it had all gone over my head, and I wasn't the only one. Eventually, Mother asked a teacher from Stradbroke Boys' School to come in and teach me the most elementary facts of algebra and geometry. After that, I got on fine.

I remember arguing about this, later on, when I was teaching and the idea came in that all teachers – even infants' teachers – would have to have a degree. It is a mistake to put someone who finds a subject very easy, to teach the young in the early stages. It seems to me that people who have had difficulties in learning are much the best to teach children who are also going to have difficulties.

Miss Haig retired as headmistress in July 1925, and was replaced by Miss Copeman, a very different cup of tea. Miss Copeman's brother was Canon Copeman of Norwich Cathedral... about whom we heard time and time again!

She was extremely religious. Great emphasis was given to studying not only the Bible, but the whole of the prayer book. We went through it with a toothcomb... the Common Service, morning prayer, evening prayer and – of course – the confirmation service. Between the ages of 11 and 18, when I left, there wasn't a year when we didn't make a study – in depth – of something in the Bible or prayer book, or both.

We'd start at 9am with assembly, at which I played the hymn and a stimulating march for people to walk out to. There'd be the Lord's Prayer and a reading from the Bible

... then a roll call of people who had to go to the office to be told off. Discipline was fairly hard. A great 'eye' was kept on us.

Every Ash Wednesday, the vicar of Yarmouth would come in and talk to us about Lent and Ash Wednesday, and what it all meant.

By now, I was improving so much that I went up into 3B and lower 4A. I was introduced to French by a real Frenchwoman, and we also had Latin to cope with, taught by Miss Smith. I can't say I shone at either. I suppose, really, I wasn't interested.

Then there were the Dawson sisters... Old Miss Dawson and Older Miss Dawson, as we thought of them. It turns out that one was 28 and the other even younger. Helen Dawson also taught Latin. We naturally called her 'Old Hell'. She was very vital, dark-haired, strong and short with intense blue eyes, very energetic – refereed hockey and netball, rushing up and down and shouting at us. She would call a spade a spade.

Her sister – Marjorie or Margaret Dawson – taught Geography, and it was hard to believe they were sisters. She was a great friend of Miss Tyler, who taught English. They shared lodgings and both of them were tall and willowy. Miss Geography Dawson had light, almost white hair. She was quietly spoken, and we used to play up a bit in her class.

She lived to a great age, and always came to the school Old Girls' lunches, or anything that was happening. She'd turn up on her sticks. She'd got so she couldn't walk without them, but she was always full of cheer and laughter – no end of jokes. We were lucky in our teachers.

At the High School, we had to play three games out of four – hockey, cricket, netball and tennis. The playground only had room for two tennis courts or a netball court. So, as there wasn't room there, we were given tickets to the recreation ground. Every Saturday morning, you had to get into Yarmouth and over to Beaconsfield Recreation Ground, where you played hockey in the winter and cricket in the summer.

It was a bit of a bind, but it did mean that all summer – with your ticket – you could also play tennis, free, all Saturday afternoon. I played for hours and hours, and often on a Sunday, too.

Cricket bored me stiff, and I had glasses. I had had measles when I was eight and it left me with an astigmatism. So I was always afraid the ball was going to hit me in the eye. But to get the free ticket, cricket had to be played.

Getting over to the recreation ground was quite a stretch. We would walk our bicycles through St Nicholas' church-yard, and we always stopped to look at one interesting tombstone on the wall just inside the gate. The old suspension bridge over the Bure had once collapsed during a celebration, when a clown in a tub drawn by swans was going under the bridge. As he approached, all the people were on one side of the bridge watching and, as he went under, they rushed across to the other side to see him come out – and the bridge collapsed. A number of people were drowned. This tombstone showed the clown and the swans, the bridge and the people in the air, falling into the river. We always stopped to look at it.

Then the next thing you met was the silk factory, and the smell of acid drops which emanated from it. You could smell it all over Yarmouth when the wind was in the north-east. It's a smell of my childhood – acid drops.

Chapter Seven

Once a year, the silk factory had a tremendous sale, and you could get odd bits of real silk ever so cheap – a sixpenny bundle, to make patchwork cushions, or buy it by the yard for sixpence or, at most, a shilling. It might just have a bad patch on one edge, or an odd thread pulled. I remember buying some beautiful green silk and making Mother a frock out of it. I suppose half of Yarmouth went to those three-day sales.

By the time we came to the Upper Fourth, we had to start thinking about the Oxford School Certificate, which involved studying the New Testament. Then, in detail, we did St Luke, the Acts of the Apostles, and St Paul's journeys.

I must have been 15 when the time came to choose, with the piano. Mother gave me the choice of either going on with it, and making a study of the piano or staying at school and doing my examinations. So I had my final piano lesson. That would have been in 1928.

I chose to stay at school and, after that, the piano didn't get practised as often as it might, but I don't think I was cut out to be a public pianist. I get too nervous when I play in public. So perhaps it was the right choice, and I enjoyed my schooldays tremendously. I wouldn't like to have left school at 15 and done nothing but music.

We moved in 1928. They bought a new house in Downing Road, freshly built, and semi-detached. About 1928, I suppose, we also had a wireless.

The year I went into the sixth form, 1929, there were six of us. It was the largest sixth form the High School had ever had; before that, there had been two. The fact that there were so few of us meant that you couldn't do exactly the A-levels you wanted to. I badly wanted to do horticulture and go to Reading, but I didn't get the chance. I knew a lot about plants – and animals, too. So it wasn't necessarily just horticulture. I would have liked to have had a small-holding, mini-agriculture, so to speak.

But the others all wanted to do French and English. I wanted to do Maths and Botany, but I was told I would have to do French and English... and I could take Maths or Botany as a subsidiary subject at what, in those days, was called 'AO' or 'AS' level. It was higher than the School Certificate, but not a full A-level. I did Botany. Needless to say, I didn't pass the French. I was more interested in playing tennis every night on the cliffs all through the summer months.

Among the six of us, there was Mary Hollowell, who afterwards became the first woman coroner in England; Joan Sayers, who was tremendously artistic; Joan Brooks, Kathleen Daniels... we were, of course, all prefects. We had to keep silence in the cloakroom. What a stupid rule! The cloakroom was frightfully crowded, and how you could keep silence I don't know, when everybody's bottom was in everybody else's way as you changed your shoes.

We were always the naughty class in school, the ones who got into rows because we weren't quiet enough. We weren't subdued enough. We ran down the stairs instead of walking. We jumped down them. But we did have extremely good exam results. Teaching has altered an awful lot. If you have a naughty class now, they are seen as being lively and needing more interesting work. In those days, we were just sort of crushed... told to be quiet or we'd be reported to the Head.

Phyllis aged 17

Chapter Eight

"The whole thing was a shock"

COLLEGE DAYS

I went to Goldsmiths College at New Cross in 1931. It was an incredibly poor area, around New Cross and Lewisham. It was all rather a horror to a country girl like me, who never imagined what a city like London was like.

There were a lot of homeless people. People were found dead in the street on winter mornings, and hustled away by the authorities before daylight to the mortuary – a quick inquest, and into a pauper's grave. A lot of that sort of thing happened. Things were hushed up. We were warned to go about in twos.

Later, in 1936, the Jarrow Marchers were to come down from the North. Those poor men! People were going out on the road and passing them pieces of bread and cups of tea as they went by, giving them cardboard and string to tie around their shoes, which had worn out. Some of them were in bare feet.

The whole thing was a shock to me. I was used to people living in tumble-down cottages with leaking roofs and no bathroom, with water from a well and farmyard smells. But this struck me as horrifying, the way people were having to live in London. It was the lack of privacy, and there was no fresh air. While you might get unwashed bodies in the country, and the smell of pigs or onions cooking, at least OUTSIDE there was fresh air. Here, everything was stuffy.

My first school practice was in Surrey Commercial Docks. At the top of Commercial Road there was a stall selling cooked peas and faggots. You'd see children carrying home two saucers – one with a couple of faggots, and one with cooked peas. That would be the midday meal for the whole family, with perhaps a bit of bread.

Then, along Commercial Road, as you went into the docks area, there were enormous, very squalid blocks of flats, back-to-back, with standpipes and communal lavatories in yards between each two blocks. Originally, they may have been quite good flats but by 1931, there was so much poverty that they had been split into separate rooms and sublet. You might have three families in each, sharing a kitchen. When I started, I used to take a deep breath in New Cross Road and hold it as long as I could. I think smells affect me more than anything.

The back of Ruby Street, at the Elephant and Castle, where some of the other girls went, was a similarly overcrowded, very poor area.

My first teaching practice was a month or six weeks, and I had opted to teach seniors. The school was three storeys high, with an iron staircase, shared lavatories and a small, shared playground. Classes had to have different playtimes, so there were always people rattling up and down the iron stairs.

The classroom was not more than 20 feet from the railway lines, on the other side. Trains went by every five minutes. The windows were so covered with soot that they didn't let in much daylight, and you could hardly see out of them. The whole school was very crowded – with up to 64 in a class, sitting in dual desks.

Nits were one of our big problems. We used to wash our hair with anti-nit soap during school practices, and comb each other's hair, looking for the monsters. Where I was teaching, the nurse came round and found that every child had them. So we marched them down to the police station, where their heads were massaged with a mixture that smelled like turps. Then all the children had their heads wrapped up in scarves, and were sent home to wash their hair.

There was also a social service sort of thing we had to do – going out about once a fortnight, taking turns, to schools in the Greenwich area. They used to re-open the schools at 6pm, and keep them open until 8pm. The children came back to school to play, because there was nothing for them at home. There were games – but everything was in a desperate state, all terribly smelly, cooped up.

Many of us went to college straight from school (what a mistake!) and, like me, without really having had anything to do with children. I had taught in Sunday school a bit, but I was totally ignorant about 'elementary' schools – as they were called. I had opted to take A-levels instead of spending my last year at school as a student teacher in an elementary school. I think I would have had much more idea what I was doing if I had done that.

At college, I lived in a hostel – Surrey Hostel. That was an extraordinary place, a three-storey house built on the side of a hill, with a huge conservatory at the back which was the dining room.

It was on the corner of Lewisham High Road and trams ran by until two in the morning, starting again at four. Occasionally, one went off the points at the junction, and there'd be a tremendous amount of shouting and shoving and clanking as the tram was got back onto the tramlines. Then, of course, the tram had an overhead runner, so there'd be all this fuss getting the tram over the points and swinging the overhead runner round on to the new wires.

Our dining room was bitterly cold in winter. I remember pease puddings, very solid, and cabbages which were likely to have caterpillars in. Generally, the food was edible... though we did once tie a piece of red cotton to a kipper's tail, and count how many times it came up for our breakfast before it was eaten.

After supper, we would play the piano, if we didn't have any work to do, and sort of dance around the edges of the tables. I played a bit... some of the jazz that I had learned from my father.

Of course, it was a female hostel. There were no mixed hostels in those days. About 45 of us lived there. There were rooms of three, two... a couple of single rooms... and two or three dormitories of six.

Goldsmiths College was rather like going into the Underground. I never remember any windows in the main hall, though I suppose it must have had some. The lavatories were tiled and Victorian, very dull.

I remember there were more than 100 Welsh miners at the college, who were getting out of the mines by doing a teaching certificate. Waiting for meals, they used to stand outside the door and sing.

As students, we were all very hard up, and there wasn't really any opportunity to earn extra money. There was so much unemployment. I think I had half-a-crown a week, and out of that I was supposed to write home once a week (though stamps were only one-and-a-half pence). We did our own washing, and dried it as best we could in the basement.

Life was very restricted. If you wanted to be out for supper, and didn't expect to be in until 10pm, you had to get permission – and then you would be let in by Miss Sheriff, the warden, who didn't exactly greet you with joy.

Miss Sheriff was a very sour person. She didn't really have much to do with the students, but sat up in her drawing room. If we were too noisy, she would ring a bell, and one of us would have to go to her room and be warned that we must make less noise. She never really appeared except at breakfast and supper time. Then she sat at the top table, and seven of us each day had to go and eat our meal with her. I think it was done in alphabetical order.

So we did at least meet her once or twice a term. But I don't remember much conversation around that table. She never asked us about our work, or what we were doing or where we were teaching, or what we were interested in ... or even where we were going at the weekend, if we had a weekend off. She seemed to have a very lonely life, and I don't think she was very fond of the students.

Despite the restrictions, they didn't stop you going out early in the morning. We would go out at six and go swimming, and get up at four to go to Covent Garden... getting back by eight for breakfast. That was exciting.

Excursions were cut to the minimum, because no one had any money. But you could get into Sadlers Wells for four pence if you were right up in the top gallery. We also went to the cinema, if we could afford it, near New Cross Station. I remember seeing '*Jack's The Boy*' with Jack Hulbert and Cicely Courtneidge. I thought it was the funniest film I had ever seen, and it had a very catchy song:

> "The flies crawl up the window,
> They crawl up two by two ..."

Then, with no television in those days, there were all the wonderful things that came from America – the cartoons.

Some weekends, I went to see the Baroness de Ville, who still lived in the same incredible flat on the other side of London where I had been taken when I was four years old... very Victorian, big rooms full of heavy furniture. The old-fashioned water closet with its willow pattern was still the same.

It was a couple of bus rides and, to me, quite expensive – 10d at least – but sometimes I stayed the night. There were a lot of her younger friends, and she gave a party occasionally. She always gave me a good meal, and did me the great favour of teaching me to play backgammon properly – a game I've enjoyed ever since.

I did start doing a degree. Then things became very difficult... and I really wasn't very clever. I wasn't really a worker. So after the first term, I gave up all idea of doing a full three-year degree and opted into the two-year diploma course, which was a blessing in the end. This meant that I did Advanced Maths (which I passed, though I never did fathom calculus), Biology (which I found very interesting), English and – of course – teaching practice.

For my second school practice, I could choose a junior or infants school. I opted for juniors because I had heard too many horrifying tales about how they had to help the infants feed at dinner time. Remember, I was not just an only child, but an only grandchild as well. I'd never held a baby.

This time, I was sent to a rather superior school – a very nice, modern building at Manor Park. Again, they were very large classes, with 60 or more pupils, but the rooms were bigger and, in juniors, we were moving away from the 'chalk and talk' era, and just beginning to get a more practical approach to teaching. I remember we made a sort of model railway out of cardboard, and we began to have children moving around in groups.

The idea now was to do something, and learn from what you were doing – though, of course, my grandfather had been doing that in the early 1900s. You see, this was the beginning of the great alteration in teaching, away from the days when it was strictly 'the 3Rs'... and anything else the head teacher happened to be interested in.

My last school practice, again with seniors, was at a brand-new school on a brand-new housing estate the other side of Lewisham. People had only just been moved there, out of the slums. The people were worried and unhappy. They hadn't got their friends near them. There was no community centre, just four shops. And there was still always this awful unemployment.

And, of course, although they now had baths, people DID keep coal in them. You could understand it. They had suddenly been put into these modern houses – with no prior training – when they had been used to living in perhaps one or two rooms, with washing facilities in the yard or washing in a basin on the table.

However, the school had been built for 600, round the sides of a square, and we did all have our own playground, plus a big assembly hall. Great advances had been made. In the school, they had built a flat – with a sitting room, kitchen, bathroom and bedroom. Each week, four of the top girls lived in the flat. They learned to clean it, lay the table, cook and wash and iron – household management. This was a tremendous advance.

I didn't really have any politics. I suppose I had been affected by the Communists to a certain degree, because our professor of mathematics was a Communist. But that was all. I mean, I had listened to the arguments around the table... endless arguments at home because my grandfather Land was a true-blue Tory, and Grandfather Chambers was a confirmed Liberal; Lloyd George was his hero. And my father, just to be awkward I'm absolutely sure, had been a Socialist.

So I had been aware of politics but I don't think it affected me. I was far more affected by the dictionary on the table, and how if I did not know the meaning of a word, it was looked up promptly... and I was made to spell it. That went on until quite a late age – I remember having to spell 'diarrhoea' several times, because I could never get it right!

But I think I had led quite a superficial life, after the age of 16 when my grandparents left Sudbourne. Even though I went down to the Surrey Commercial Docks on school practice, and afterwards taught there for a month before coming home... I was, I suppose, appalled by the conditions, but it never struck me that maybe I could do something about it myself.

I mean, I just accepted it. I hated it, but by the time I got back to the hostel, I had forgotten. The day-to-day routine of the college didn't give you much time to think deeply. I don't think any of us did. You were more interested in the next dance, or getting through the next teaching practice.

Phyllis College Girl

Phyllis aged 21, just before she went on her 'Grand Tour'

Chapter Nine

"That was really where I met Ted"

COLLEGE DAYS OVER

After I left college in June 1933, the first two or three years, I was out nearly every evening.

If I didn't go out, I used to have friends in and we used to play auction bridge and all sorts of games. I always had plenty of company, though I think I was still very naïve.

My generation was still suffering from a lack of young men after the first world war. It did leave an enormous gap. When you went to a dance, you'd have at least two-thirds women there, and the girls danced together. I had started going to dances about 1930 – a Post Office dance with my parents – and it had been the same story at college.

So, you see, there was a very good chance you were going to be left on the shelf, as we said in those days. I was very anxious. I was an only child, and an only grandchild on both sides. Perhaps because of that, I had always wanted a large family. I wanted five children. You see, I spent so much time as a child with dogs and grandparents and the occasional aunt.

A lot of us were hoping, at some time, to get married and have children, and the reality is that, of my girlhood friends – the ones I played tennis and went to dances with – about half got married, and half didn't. If somebody came courting and took an interest, you naturally were pleased, and took an interest, too. I had two men-friends. One was a farmer from Northamptonshire who my grandfather did his best to put me off, saying: "Look at the number of thistles in his field!"

Then, I had been going out with a Roman Catholic. He was a great dancer. We used to go dancing two or three evenings a week, but before we went dancing on Fridays, I would have to wait while he went to confession.

Unfortunately, his family didn't welcome me because they were very strict. In the end he became a priest, and later was one of those priests who refused to take the service in English.

By this age, I had become... very practical in outlook. My mother, too, saw people with a very practical eye. She'd had the war years, with my father away, and not much money. I didn't exactly confide in my mother, but we would converse sometimes.

Grandma, too, was a very strong-minded woman who saw things from a practical angle. At one time, she'd had to really take charge, and stop my Grandfather Land from taking too much alcohol, stop him going out in the evening or having beer in the house. You see – my grandfather had taken on a very big job – with 30 keepers before the war – and he was supposed to be the boss.

I suppose, to get out and talk in a pub was a relief but, you see, you mustn't do that if you're in a position of authority on a feudal estate. You might be saying what you shouldn't, and it might be repeated.

Realism? Practicality? I suppose it often seems cold. It wasn't as cold-blooded as it sounds.

Anyway, once I returned from college, I had singing lessons; it was one of my extravagances... a very cheap extravagance by today's standards!

I had joined the Yarmouth Operatic and Dramatic Society as one of the chorus. We did a lot of Gilbert and Sullivan... The Yeoman of the Guard, The Mikado, The Gondoliers. I also joined the Philharmonic for the Triennial Festival. Yarmouth had a branch, a choir, and periodically we came up to Norwich to practise with the Norwich choir.

I went to dressmaking classes at the art school at least once a week, making frocks for my mother and myself. Tuesday was dance class, learning all the new dances – tangos! Thursday, a lot of us would go to Good's Dance Hall at the Pier Hotel in Gorleston – Evelyn, Madge and Mary.

That is where I really met Ted.

I had seen him here and there, in buses and at naturalists' meetings, just to say 'hello' or 'good morning', seen him at church. He was an object of interest in Gorleston – and, of course, there he had been, at 18, causing the revival of Yarmouth Naturalists' Society, which had collapsed during the war, going on platforms, giving talks and leading visits and excursions.

We all knew him.

I suppose, strictly speaking, I had first met Ted, to talk to, when I was 18 and at college. I had a science project to do during the summer – biology – and we were staying at St Olave's, as usual. I chose to study 'the plants of the rond, cliff and marsh'.

I found this marvellous marsh sowthistle blooming, 10ft high. It has since become extremely common, but I hadn't been to naturalists' meetings while I was at college and so I didn't know that in those days, it was desperately rare, a protected species, and this was the only marsh in Norfolk or Suffolk where it could be found. I met Ted and his friend Mr Rumbelow on the marsh. They were both very helpful but, I learned years later, I was being watched carefully. They were afraid I was one of these plant specialists who might dig it up and try to sell it.

Anyhow, one night he turned up at the Pier Hotel, looking rather lonely. Ted was not keen on dancing, but I think his mother had decided he ought to go. She thought he was concentrating too much on natural history and the museum, and was not socialising. He was sitting all alone. I started talking to him. He didn't really know anyone else – and me only to say 'hello' to.

We started going out after that. I suppose we'd meet and have a walk up and down the beach, have a cycle ride to Belton or Ashby around the lanes, perhaps take a picnic. From the start, we got on very well.

The first time he took me home... I suppose we had been talking to each other for six months by then, and meeting at various botany and natural history occasions... Ted produced a dead bat, and asked if I would hold it. It was still warm. It had only just died, and he was picking mites off it with a pair of forceps and dropping them into a tube. I don't know whether it was a test, to see if I was able to do that without actually regurgitating. But, well... I wasn't shocked. I was interested.

I can think of several of my friends who would have said 'That's enough!' and gone off to find somebody else. But I'd been brought up to be interested in nature – not in such a meticulous, fine way of looking at things, but the broader outline. I appreciated the countryside.

Anyhow, I met his mother – and took to her at once, a dear woman.

Of course, as soon as Ted took me home, his father found out I played the piano. So I would be requested to play and the old man would sing. He had a beautiful voice.

Ted and I used to sing duets in our early days – "*What Are The Wild Waves Saying?*", all those Victorian songs – at our family parties.

Ted and I were engaged in 1936 and, really, we were good company for each other. We used to do a lot of cycling together, and visit fens. I would perhaps have a book and sit and read while he was poking about, finding fungi and insects. It wasn't that I wasn't interested. I was quite happy to be shown what he had found, but I would rather sit in the sun and look at the view than take part in the botanising and biology.

Sometimes we came to Wheatfen – where Ted, of course, had already been coming since he met the owner, Captain Cockle, in about 1928. Ted had produced his first paper about Wheatfen Broad – an investigation into its plants, published in the Transactions of the Norfolk and Norwich Naturalists Society in 1934. By this time – in 1936 – he already had a reputation in the village as 'this peculiar man who comes out here and looks for things'.

It must have been about that time that there was the first BSBI gathering that I joined in – the Botanical Society of the British Isles – and there were two boats. Ted took one and I took the other. Somebody spotted a Marsh Fern, and said: "Ooh! Look!" and they all leapt up and rushed from one side of the boat to the other. You see, they weren't allowed to pick a plant... but they had to touch it before they could write it on their lists.

So I shouted: "Sit down, sit down!" Then we had to pull the boat in so that, one at a time, all the people who didn't have the wretched thing on their lists could touch it.

But, you see – what is interesting is that this was the very start of the modern attitude to conservation. Not long before, they would have all taken a piece to dry and stick in their herbarium folders. It was a significant change.

***

My first teaching post had been at Stradbroke Road, from 1933 until 1935.

I don't think I was a wonderful teacher. When you first start, you are rather anxious and very worried – not only if the head teacher is looking through the doorway. I think most of what you learn, in teaching, is through experience. And for the first two years, in those days, you had to remember that although you might have passed your written college certificate, you hadn't been registered.

I had 64 children in my first class. You literally didn't have time – if somebody couldn't read – to give them much attention or help them with the elementary moves.

Joe May, who had been my first headmaster when I was a child at the Edward Worlledge, was by now the first Chief Education Officer in Yarmouth – what would now be called the Director of Education. He used to drop in and chat to you, and see how you were getting on, in your first two years – and cast his eye over the school generally.

The Education Office expanded quite quickly, and eventually there were Organisers for different subjects who were in and out of the schools like yoyos, carrying ideas from one to another. It was useful, because you always learned something fresh from them.

In 1935, at Easter, I had been ill and away from school for three months – first with mumps and then tonsillitis. When I came out of hospital, I went on a cruise – a fortnight for £13. We went to Lisbon, Casa Blanca, Madeira. We were supposed to call at Gibraltar, but the Spanish Civil War was on. It wasn't a good idea.

From 1936 to 1938, I taught at Greenacre School. Gorleston was poor, but when I got over the water to Greenacre, I really met poverty in the face. It was appalling. The classes were divided into As and Bs. I had the 11-plus B class, the first entry into the school. The more capable children had been siphoned off into high school, grammar school and the A class.

So there were some nice, cheerful children at the top of my class who could probably have gone into the A class, if there had been room, and who would answer questions and get on, to a certain extent, by themselves.

Then, at the other end of the class, you'd got perhaps three or four who... well, they had managed to come right through infants and juniors and learned literally nothing.

These really would be 'special needs' or – in today's speech
– 'statemented' children. When I could spare the time, I'd
take two or three of them in a little group, and put something on the blackboard for the others... perhaps ask them
to draw a map.

I sometimes had group reading (with groups of eight and
a child who really could read as the leader) but, with so
many groups, the noise was tremendous!

By 1937, the main topic on the radio was Chamberlain and
the Germans, and what they were doing ... and the Russians,
and the dangers there. It was a distressing period. There
would be broadcasts of Hitler's speeches. Although Ted
and I didn't speak German, it sounded... very vituperative.

We were married on October 8th 1938. People did not
rush into marriage in those days. You waited until you'd
got enough to buy a bit of furniture and rent a house.
There were no mortgages, then. But we had been lucky.
Ted's father bought a little house for us at the bottom of
Long John Hill, down by The Cock at Lakenham for – I
think – £455. We paid him £1 a week rent, but he bought
it in our name.

So we were married at Gorleston Parish Church.

I refused to have the choir, much to Ted's disgust. The choir
wanted to sing because, of course, Ted was still a member,
and had been in it since 1919 – first as a soprano, then a
high tenor and later a baritone. It was a lovely choir – all
male, of course. Well, officially. In fact, there was one
woman, Mrs Richards. She was the cousin of the organist,
and was allowed to sit behind a screen and sing contralto
– but she was never allowed to show herself!

So the choir wanted to sing, but I didn't want a frightfully posh wedding, and I'd seen choirboys sniggering at weddings, and all that sort of thing. I just didn't fancy it somehow.

Ted chose the hymns – and chose to have The Dance of the Sugar Plum Fairy for us to come out with... very unusual but very nice. Evelyn, my chief friend from high school days, was my bridesmaid. I was 25, and Ted was 29.

We went straight from the reception to our new house, and planned to have a week's holiday in Guernsey in the summer of 1939.

I suppose getting married was the next big change – and having to adjust, because Ted was just as... unaware of the real world as I was. I mean, he was immersed in natural history. And right from the beginning, Ted and I had very different natures. I suppose Ted and I got together through a common interest in natural history and the church. Ted had always had a very earnest belief in God and the Christian church, but he began to lose his faith in Christianity... to feel that 'religious' people might only be 'religious' on Sundays, and that Christianity might be getting away from Christ's spirit – his embracing the whole world in a caring spirit.

Anyhow, before we got married, Ted had said to me: "Ever since I was 19, I have only missed one or two church services, and I have no intention of going into a fresh parish and joining the choir and attending church every Sunday".

In a sense, that suited me, too. So we used to go cycling. We sometimes went to church, but we were getting away from churchgoing regularly. I don't think I went to church again until John was two...

Our first house was small, and so exceedingly draughty that the wind blew the carpet up. Even when it was tacked down, you could see the carpet rising and falling.

There was a tiny dining-room which became Ted's den, but it was not nearly big enough for him. So books used to creep out of his den, and spread along the top of the piano, then along the keyboard. I used to push them back into his den!

The kitchen was equally small. Outside, there was a hut for our bicycles, and we dug a trench to keep home-made wine in. We didn't have a lot of money. Ted earned £5 a week. But we would go out to the Maddermarket Theatre – with a cheap season ticket.

We used to go cycling in the country and gather black-berries, and make blackberry wine, hawthorn wine, jams and jellies. We were very industrious.

We felt as though we were living in the country, in Lakenham. We had a quarter of an acre of garden. Sandy Lane really was a sandy lane then. The cliff in front of our house – which has council housing all over it now – was still a meadow. There was a pond and, beyond it, footpaths to Arminghall. We were the last house in the city.

So when we were asked what we would like for a wedding present, Ted had said he wanted some gorse bushes, sweet-briar bushes and some tamarisk. We made a fence around the garden of sweetbriar and tamarisk, with gorse bushes in the front. Instead of a square of grass, we had a square of clover with beautiful red blossoms. We made a gravel patch, with flowers and tiny irises in it, with early spring flowers and other things. We worked very hard – I made a very satisfactory pond, with all sorts of irises around the edge.

I had had to give up work once we were married. In the Thirties, there was such terrible unemployment that that was the rule for women – unless they were doctors. But I did a certain amount of babysitting at night, and children came and played in the garden if their parents were busy.

In June 1939, Ted and I went to Guernsey for a holiday and had a marvellous fortnight. Kept a bottle of sloe gin and a bottle of cherry brandy under the bed, you know.

But it was when the Germans were getting ready. We saw two or three boatloads of these strong, healthy Germans in their shorts – looking everywhere, inspecting everything, buying all the postcards, all the maps. It's no wonder Jersey, Guernsey and Alderney fell so fast when the invasion came.

But, as yet, all of this was in the future...

Ted and Phyllis wedding 1938

Phyllis at Somerleyton 1938

Phyllis in a boat 1940

Ted and Phyllis wedding photo l-r Jimmy Ellis, Lucy Chambers, Martin Ellis, Ted Ellis, Phyllis, Evelyn Crannas, Ada Chambers, Alice Ellis, Jack Chambers.

Ted and Phyllis newlywed 1938

E R

I WISH TO MARK, BY THIS PERSONAL MESSAGE, my appreciation of the service you have rendered to your Country in 1939.

In the early days of the War you opened your door to strangers who were in need of shelter, & offered to share your home with them.

I know that to this unselfish task you have sacrificed much of your own comfort, & that it could not have been achieved without the loyal co-operation of all in your household.

By your sympathy you have earned the gratitude of those to whom you have shown hospitality, & by your readiness to serve you have helped the State in a work of great value.

Elizabeth R

Mrs. L. R. Chambers.

Message from Queen to Lucy Rebecca Chambers

Chapter Ten

"We'd lost our home but how wonderful to be alive!"

WAR YEARS

War finally broke out in September 1939, when we had been married a little less than a year. Ted volunteered for the Navy but, at the medical examination, they found bad patches on his lungs. They told him to go home, live quietly, and said he would be lucky to live five years. Well, that wasn't very good news to come home with...

So we dug our Anderson shelter – sandbags in front and a hillock of earth on top, with a couple of bunks inside. It was only 4ft 6in long, so you had to sleep with your knees up. I spent quite a lot of time in that small shelter, while Ted was out three nights a week – sometimes more – fire watching or on first aid duty.

Once the war started, we weren't supposed to go to Great Yarmouth. They were trying to keep people away from the coast because they were expecting an invasion. My father's post office at Yarmouth had been dished out with wooden guns and pepper in case of the invasion. Packets of pepper! But it really wasn't very funny, was it?

But in November, Mother came up to see me, and wanted to see my doctor. She was very worried because her stomach was getting larger, and she was beginning to feel very ill. The doctor found that, indeed, she had cancer. The hospital consultant ordered an operation but there was a dearth of beds; they were keeping several wards empty because at any moment we expected bombs to fall, which – despite a lot of air raid warnings – hadn't really started yet. Then in January 1940, there was a terrible flu epidemic. Half the hospital staff were off, and people were getting pneumonia. This again delayed Mother's operation. She eventually went in at the beginning of February but they had left it too late. All they could do was send her home to me.

She hadn't been told she had cancer and that it was final. I knew, and my father knew. We emptied Ted's tiny den because she was bedridden now and we put the spare bed in there. We stuck muslin on the windows so that if there was a bomb glass splinters wouldn't fly.

Father used to come up every weekend and help to look after her, which gave me some free time to do the shopping. He wasn't allowed to retire. He was too young for early retirement, the war being on.

Mother was in that bed from the end of February. The doctor came twice a day, in the later stages, and a nurse came to help me bathe her. She got so that she couldn't keep anything down, not even water. In the end, she had to be told she was dying and her remark was: "Oh, my poor Jack!"

She died on June 17 – the night France fell. A dreadful day. She hadn't eaten anything for weeks. She was 58.

It was the same night that Dad's dear friend was killed on Haddiscoe Bridge. He was returning from a late shift at the post office, and an LDV – a local defence volunteer, later called the Home Guard – on the bridge said: "Halt! Who goes there?" He wound down the car window to speak to the man, and the gun went off, killing him.

The LDV had his finger on the trigger, when it shouldn't have been. But everyone had the jitters, you know, expecting to find German spies everywhere.

We had Mother's cremation very quickly because I didn't see how I could have her lying dead in the house and – as everyone thought – bombs imminent.

During the war, we grew our own vegetables. I got half a dozen cross-bred chickens and kept rabbits. Eventually, I became secretary of the Lakenham Rabbit and Poultry Society.

Then there were afternoons at St Andrew's Hall, in Norwich, which St John's and the WRVS had organised between them as a canteen for all the forces. They could buy a cup of tea or Camp coffee... and there we were, at the back, making hundreds and hundreds of sausage rolls and pancakes with treacle... like a production line.

The scene in the kitchens reminded me – though I hadn't yet seen it – of the Charlie Chaplin film Modern Times. We were allowed a certain amount of fat and sugar. Flour wasn't rationed at that time, but the treacle used to run out sometimes. I was there from 1939 until 1941.

I had become friendly with George and Audrey Rogers, who ran the grocery shop at the bottom of Long John Hill. Because a married woman wasn't allowed to work, I helped them at the shop. That was in the days when butter arrived in a large lump, and had to be cut up into two-ounce pieces for rations. Sugar came in a sack and had to be weighed out into blue bags. Cheese had to be cut. So I used to go down to the shop, and help, weighing things up, doing the shelves... and then came the ration coupons!

With the advent of rationing, you had these coupons, which, at first, you had to cut out separately. If someone wanted a pound of sugar, you had to take a thing the size of... well, not even as big as a postage stamp. Then they all had to be counted at the end of the week, to see how much sugar, butter, marg, cheese and whatever you had coupons for. They were different colours, so they all had to be put into separate piles and counted. You had a mountain of coupons to count.

We had a lot of night disturbances, and sirens – plenty of scares. I remember doing a lot of knitting, sitting in air raid shelters, waiting for the 'all clear', when I was caught in town. It made people very friendly. You chatted, and you always had a book with you – not that the light was very good, especially later when it would flicker as the bombs landed or even go out. But at first, there were just a lot of false alarms.

Finally, the very first bombs on Norwich were on a sunny afternoon in August or September 1940. I was playing tennis. I was pregnant by then. When the siren started shrieking, there was no time to do anything – and no shelters there anyway. This plane came over, very low. There were a couple of explosions, and then it departed hastily. Boulton and Paul's had been hit and, as we looked, on the updraught from the fire, there was a pillar of smoke and paper documents. The wind was in our direction, and a lot of the documents fell on the tennis court. We picked up as many as we could. I don't know why. We just felt we should rescue them. I don't remember playing tennis again after that. There was too much else to do.

On April 2nd 1941, John was born... with shrapnel flying in all directions! I had gone down to Heigham Grove Hall, a nursing home which was wonderful, run by the council. It was a big room with big windows and, as they were delivering John, Thorpe Station was attacked by a German bomber, which then came down the road, firing everywhere. I just remember the matron getting one of the hospital screens, as the plane came towards us, and holding it up in front of the window! I don't suppose it would have stopped very much, but that's just the kind of thing people do.

When John was five weeks old, our house was bombed. It was one of the first bombings of a private house in Norwich. Despite our shelter, we were indoors that night. The bombs fell at the back, between the allotments and the swimming pool. All the ceilings came down, and the windows blew in. Fortunately, I had pasted net on to the downstairs windows, so there were no glass splinters.

We'd lost our home... but how wonderful to be alive!

We were offered somewhere to stay, but we decided not to move out – because people were breaking into houses. It was mended straight away. I think by eight in the morning, the tiles were off the roof, and we had a dozen men running everywhere, putting up paper ceilings and putting the doors back on their hinges, putting black stuff over the windows with a transparent strip at the top to let a little light in.

So we carried on, but I got fed up with the dirt, and the cracks in the walls, the darkness, the ceilings going up and down when the wind blew, sleeping in the air raid shelter. In August, Ted had a week's holiday coming up, and I had been very cross with him because he hadn't planned anything. So I said: "When you come home tonight, you WILL have arranged some sort of holiday." Well, he rang up at dinner time and said: "We're catching the 8.15pm train tonight to Wales."

He'd got this address at Llyn Ogwen from somebody who had brought a fungus in. We had to change trains at two in the morning, and we arrived at Aberystwyth at 8.15 – a 12-hour journey! We got a taxi to Llyn Ogwen. They didn't really expect us to arrive as early as that, but they made us very welcome.

So there we were, trudging up Llyn Ydwel with a blue carrycot. We were rather tired, so we left the carrycot halfway. Eventually, we were sitting on the summit and we could see the carrycot – a spot of blue in the distance, ever so tiny. Then Ted looked up and said: "Oh! Those are ravens. Hope they don't pluck the baby's eyes out!" I was down that hill in half a minute. I don't think I've gone down a steep hill so fast in my life.

It was a gorgeous holiday. We trudged all over. The sun shone. There were no sirens, no planes. There was butter, cream, lovely food... lots of mutton. Then, of course, we came back – a 13-hour journey, and the train crowded with soldiers. And as we got in to the railway station, the sirens were going.

I began MAGNA – the Mutual Aid Good Neighbours Association – in Lakenham.

There had been a lot of trouble, that year, and I found that people were queuing up at the City Hall in coats and dressing gowns, and anything they could rescue, waiting for help. They had lost their ration books and identity cards. It was very disorganised. Nobody was doing anything about it. So I was allowed to open Lakenham School as a centre. The WRVS came and brought clothes. Some of the school cooks came and made meals. We had a man from City Hall come in to issue clothing coupons and things.

I'm afraid I did it off my own bat. After I'd been running this centre at Lakenham for about a week, they sent down a man from London. He was very cross because he said I hadn't kept the right books and so on. I remarked that I had been too busy to keep books. There was a row, and he read me the Riot Act and I'm afraid I told him he was constipated with red tape.

Then my friend, the parson at Stoke Holy Cross, phoned me and said there were a lot of cottages in his neighbour-hood where they would be glad to take evacuees from Norwich. I went down to the bus station, and they'd got a couple of buses with no windows left in them. So we used them to move the people out to Stoke Holy Cross.

One of the ministers from London came out because she wanted to see what MAGNA was doing – and she wasn't best pleased. I got told off for taking people out to the villages. I said if she'd watched people going by my house and sleeping under hedges where and when they could, she might alter her mind.

The following June, 1942, we had a whole canister of fire-bombs. Instead of breaking up in the air, the canister just fell in two halves – one in the garden and one in the house. Just our luck! We had a bathful of water ready upstairs, as people were advised to do, but the fire was too intense. We didn't stand a chance of rescuing anything from upstairs. Later we found, sorting through the wreckage, that a mirror upstairs had been melted into a ball of glass in the intense heat.

That was the end of me doing things for other people much. I'd got the baby, and I was fully occupied. So I really only started MAGNA. Afterwards it was taken over by... someone who kept the books better! In any case, things calmed down. I suppose they'd got better organised by that time.

We now stayed with friends, the Coes, at Lakenham Hall for three months, before renting rooms at Broads Farm, Rockland, in September. In early December 1942, we moved again, taking rooms at The Rookery, Hellington.

In the summer of 1943, I was required to go to Langley Junior School – opposite the Cantley factory – as a supply teacher. John, now two, spent the days with a neighbour who had a four-year-old daughter. They had had a string of bombs in the marshes. I found that every time a plane went over, the children disappeared underneath the desks ... just like that!

At last, in August 1943, we bought a semi-detached cottage at Brundall, on Blofield Road, overlooking the Braydeston marshes.

Water was from a well, with a pail closet. There were three bedrooms, and two living rooms (one of which became Ted's den again). The kitchen had a full-sized bath in it, under the window! It just fitted in, with a shallow sink over one end. There was an open fire, with grids on it to boil saucepans, and a Dutch oven in the wall. The garden was quite big, with several apple trees, a big plum tree, room to grow vegetables and a nice big run for my six chickens and my rabbits.

I took John on the bicycle down to Blofield Church for evening service sometimes.

It would have been alright if the house had had more sun, but the living room was on the north side, and the sun never got round to it. I became very depressed, especially in the double summertime.

By this time, I was pregnant again, but I had had a disagreement with the doctor. In December 1943, our next-door neighbour's baby, little John, had a slight operation, which was done at home. I was asked to go and hold the child's arms and legs still while the operation was done, in the meantime the district nurse gave the anaesthetic. The boy's mother, Mrs Brigham, didn't feel she could do it.

I went across and I remember feeling sick, kneeling holding the child's hands and legs... there was quite a lot of blood, and the smell of the anaesthetic... Anyway, when it was over, and the child was bandaged up, the doctor looked at me and said: "You haven't been back to the surgery."

I said: "No, and I'm not coming either, if you're going to talk to me like that. I've booked up at the nursing home, so that's alright."

However, he examined me. Afterwards, I gave him tea on half the table in Ted's den, with all the cardboard boxes around us... all Ted's fungus collection in shoeboxes, and his microscope standing there on the table. The doctor was very interested. He enjoyed his cake, and began asking questions about Ted. He must have decided we weren't so bad as we looked, and after that he was always friendly.

I spent three months teaching juniors – from eight to 14 – at Strumpshaw School before Easter in 1944. I cycled, taking John – now three – on the back of my bicycle, and he was dumped in the infants' room.

Mary was born on June 9 at home, despite the plans to go into a nursing home. The doctor sent me in early, then said I wasn't ready and asked me to go back home again. When I got home that night, I went into labour, and Mary was eventually born at seven in the morning. Poor Ted was cycling up and down the village. A taxi wasn't available. So then he went down to Blofield to fetch a doctor while our next-door neighbour rushed to find the district nurse. Mary was a lovely baby, but she was blue when she was born.

Next day, Ted went to fetch his mother to look after me. After that, it wasn't easy to go to church, because of feeding the baby, but I did still occasionally take John.

I knew Wheatfen well by this time. We kept a punt, and used to come down to Wheatfen, land on what is called Blake's Marsh and walk up to Smee Loke, to see our friends the Cockles... first with John, who was three or four, and later with Mary in a carrycot in the punt. I'd carry her in a sling over the marshes. On other occasions, we cycled, coming across the ferry from Brundall.

Once, on our way, we heard this enormous explosion and, when we got here, there were wires, springs and bits of metal all over the road. Several bungalows in Surlingham had lost their roofs, and there were one or two trees down. It was one of the first rockets (V2s) that had come down without exploding properly, so the Army was terribly excited about the prospect of examining it.

By the time we arrived, soldiers were in the road, picking up all the bits with great care. Not a bit was missed and everything was charted.

I was still gleaning for corn. At Brundall, there was a farmer who had a lot of cornfields next to the railway, which was still steam in those days. He had a special insurance for those fields because, nine times out of ten, sparks from the engines landed in the corn. You nearly always had one field – and probably two – catching fire in a dry season. Then the insurance would pay up, and anyone who wanted to could go and glean there.

Well, I was well away. With chickens to feed, I could get a good lot of corn. I remember before Mary was born taking John, who was two-and-a-half, I suppose. Then, soon after, I was going down again, having to get John and my sacks and Mary over the stiles and gates and things.

In 1944, there was a lot of Army activity on the roads, endless traffic going south. We knew something was going on. It was all very hush-hush, and we were told we couldn't have visitors coming to stay in Norfolk, unless they were relatives. There was a bit of a scare about German spies.

So when my friend Alice came to stay along with her three children, I had to say she was my sister. Alice arrived before Mary was a fortnight old. So then there were five children. Her John was five, her Margaret was four and Valerie was 14 months. The summer was very hot and our well, though it was very deep, was shared by eight houses. It became so short of water that when you put your bucket down, it came up half full of sand and shingle.

My rainwater tubs gave out, with all the washing, but we were able to economise by letting them play in the garden naked while we did our modicum of housework in the mornings.

There was a nice dyke about a quarter of a mile away, with water good enough for washing, and my father found an old watercart, but its wheels didn't have any tyres. You couldn't get tyres. So he made rope grommets – very nicely made, too. A lot of trouble it took, because they needed a proper splice and they had to fit well.

But, of course, they weren't air-filled tyres, so by the time we'd wheeled our cart uphill to where we lived, going bumpity, bumpity bump... we'd lost quite a lot of water. Never mind, we got enough to bathe the children and do the washing.

In fact, big John used to look askance at the bathwater when it was his turn, because we did it in strict age rotation. The baby was first, and more water was added for each of the others. So by the time it was big John's turn, it was getting... a little dim. He had to put up with it.

Alice was sad because her husband wasn't with her. He had to stay in London. But it was a happy time for us, in many ways. We enjoyed the hot weather.

The local farmer wouldn't let us have any extra milk for the visitors because – although it wasn't really rationed – we weren't supposed to have visitors. He stuck to this. So every day, one of us went up to the Enochs, who lived a mile away and kept goats. We got a gallon of goats' milk. When we got home, we would arrange a line of children in front of us – not only the four older ones from our house, but Peggy and little John from next door and, if it was holiday time, sometimes their Joan as well. Then we'd go down the line, putting a teaspoon of cod liver oil in each mouth, followed by a teaspoon of the orange that the government dished out, followed by a drink of goats' milk. Then we would pack up a lunch with lemonade and a Thermos flask, and we went over the hills towards

Braydeston church. As you got towards the church, there was the remains of a sandpit. The ground sloped sharply down from the path and at the bottom, there was a stream good enough to paddle and play and splash in, so the children could slide down the cliff, and do what they liked, while we gossiped or read books and I fed the baby.

When the baby became restless, we went home and cooked supper ready for Ted to come home.

If the weather wasn't good enough, then we all came inside and played jumping off the couch, and snakes and ladders, and hide and seek... all sorts of games that we concocted.

I used to go shopping in Brundall on a bicycle, with John on the seat behind and Mary in the basket... a big bag of shopping on each handlebar. Very dangerous. It's a good job there wasn't traffic like there is now.

We used to get parcels of clothing from America. In one of those was a lovely white imitation fur coat that exactly fitted Mary. She was about 14 months old.

I remember Ted telling me that if I wanted to go and see this film, *Arsenic and Old Lace*, I could go on a Thursday – his afternoon off – and he would look after John, aged four, and Mary, aged 16 months. They were spotless when they went out... ears clean, faces clean. When I met them at the station afterwards, I never saw two such tramps in my life! He'd given them chocolate, and there was chocolate all over their faces and all down the front of their clothes – especially Mary in her nice white fur coat. And not only had he given them chocolate, he'd also taken them around the fire station which, in those days, had a long brick wall around it, three feet high. They'd been crawling along the top of the wall.

And, of course, when we got on the train, we got into the same carriage with the Misses Colman. I always wondered – whatever did they think of Ted's wife, and their filthy children! I don't think he ever looked after them again after that.

John and Martin in a boat 1948

Mary, Martin and John at Wheatfen 1948

Russell, John, Pam Ellis, Mary, Martin Ellis, Phyllis, Martin 1948

Ellis family at Wheatfen 1960

Mary, Suzie, Phyllis and Lucy 1955

Chapter Eleven

"We have always lived with hornets"

WHEATFEN

I first came to Wheatfen in 1936, before we were engaged, and I thought it was like coming home – the nearest thing to the Sudbourne of my childhood.

Here was the wood, with birches and bracken, a house – made from two cottages put together – standing by itself a quarter of a mile from the nearest neighbour. Here were the marshes, the garden and the birds singing. I thought what a wonderful place it was – as, indeed, did Ted, although he regarded it from the point of view of a naturalist, the variety of things here. From that time, I wanted to live here.

The Cockles became our friends. We visited often.   We stayed for weekends. We camped.

Then, in November 1945, there was a knock on the door one dark, dreary night – and it was Russell Sewell, who worked for the Cockles. He had come to say that Captain Cockle had just died in hospital. Soon we were given an opportunity to rent Wheatfen for 10 years.

Now, just about then, Ted had been offered a wonderful opportunity to go to Baghdad – to plan, equip and run a new natural history museum. We would have had servants and a bungalow up in the hills. He was also offered, at about that time, a promising job in Richmond at what was then the Imperial Institute of Mycology. Although he wanted to do mycology, at Richmond he would have done nothing but mycology.

Here, the rent was quite high, and we would be on a repairing lease, taking on a place that had been bomb damaged. Water would be from a well, with no electricity and only wood fires.

So, of course... we couldn't consider anything else!

Wheatfen was what we wanted. It was the place where Ted had already done so much work. More was known about Wheatfen than about any similar place in the British Isles. There were more species of plants, insects and fungi here than at Wicken Fen. So we signed the lease.

We would have just enough in our bank-book, after we sold the house at Brundall, to pay for the 10-year lease here. Ted's wages had not risen during the war, of course. He was still on £5 a week. So it was rather daring of us to take this on... especially with three young children. (Martin was now six weeks old, having been born on December 14.)

Ted had to move in quickly, early in January 1946, because although the war had finished by now, there were a lot of homeless people in the countryside, or families making do in small caravans. The war had left a great shortage of housing. So people were just walking into any empty houses they found, and squatting ... and then it was practically impossible to get rid of them. In fact, the first night Ted spent at Wheatfen, people came looking in the windows, and saying: "Here's an empty house – let's move in." He was there, of course, so it was fine.

I had to stay at the Brundall house for the same reason.

Fortunately, we had a quick sale. A gentleman was so keen to buy that he took the cash out of his pocket, and offered it to me there and then – £800! I told him he'd have to at least go and see a lawyer, which he did – but we moved within three days. I said: "We'll clear out at once and you can move in whenever you like – whether we've finished with contracts or not".

I must say, it was a bit of a facer, but you do what you have to do.

It was late January. I remember the rain. It rained and rained the day we moved in properly. We arrived in an open lorry with a tilt over it, which was all we could get at short notice. The lane was flooded, and outside the house was a sea of mud. So soon the inside was covered in mud as well... but how happy we were!

Dear old Mrs Mack, from the village, came wading up the lane in gumboots and a mackintosh – she must have been 70 – with a large, home-cured ham, a big jar of bottled plums, a pound of sugar and a large piece of home-made butter. She said: "I thought it might make you a nice supper, dear."

Rationing was still in force, and it was the best present I had had since before the war.

Well, it continued to pour in torrents, through January... all through February... March. It seems that it rained every day, in my memory.

Life wasn't easy. There was no coal, or cut wood for fuel. I discovered a fallen trunk and – I can picture the scene now – there was little John, not quite five, at one end of a cross-cut saw and me at the other. Between us, with great labour, we would saw a piece off. Then I would chop it up with an axe, so we could have a fire and some warmth in the house. It was a very frugal life, but in the spring we grew our own vegetables... and it was fun!

The weather was bitterly cold, the first few winters and the house was damp. A pair of shoes left upstairs would grow mould in a week. The repairs needed to the house were quite major. It had had bombs all around it, and ceilings in the upstairs rooms were hanging in strips. Every time you closed the door, there was a shower of plaster!

You see, although Surlingham was not a chosen target, German planes would sometimes jettison left-over bombs as they turned back towards the coast from Norwich. There had been a landmine dropped in Rockland Broad, a big bomb on Home Marsh, there'd been butterfly bombs dropped all around – including in the wood – and two smaller bombs on Old Mill Marsh, next to Penguin Dyke.

Still, in spite of all the drawbacks, I was delighted to be here. We could go out on the water whenever we liked, and Ted in October started writing these wonderful articles – and they were wonderful, those first articles, looking back on them. They were magical.

And we were free. We were very, very busy. It was hard work. But we could go out at midnight, and walk around. We could do what we liked – have a bonfire, if we wanted.

There was a tap in the kitchen, with a semi-rotary pump, which threw up half a pint at a time. You turned on the tap, and pumped like mad. Of course, on winter mornings, you'd find the pump frozen solid. So first you had to light a Primus... put it underneath to thaw the pump... then take

the top off the tap and thaw that. It was quicker to go outside
and put a pail down the well on a string!

Ted was leaving home at, say, quarter to eight, and getting
home at 5.30 or 6pm. He worked all Saturdays, and at least
a half day Sunday once a month, just getting Thursday afternoons off. But I was young and I was strong, and I'd been
used to a laborious life.

There was also a bathroom upstairs, with two large water
tanks in the roof, and a very big Primus that could heat
about 10 gallons. Quite often, the bathroom was the warmest
room in the house! But to fill those tanks... once again, there
was a pump. You had to pump and pump and pump for what
seemed like forever. It took about three-quarters of an hour.

Unless we had visitors, I used to carry the water upstairs
in pails. Again, it was easier.

After the war, for several years I kept a couple of pigs
because you could kill a pig and the government would pay
for it, and take half. It was a cheap way of getting meat.

When we moved in, there was just an old Valor Perfection
two-burner paraffin stove, years and years old. Its pipes were
all sweating paraffin and it stank. I thought the kitchen
ceiling had been painted black. In fact, when I came to wash
it, it was soot!

The old stove was so objectionable that I just took it and
threw it in a pit – thinking I could go into town and buy
another. But – of course – this was 1946, and there weren't
any stoves to buy. I walked all around the town, but none
had been made during the war.

So from then until May, I cooked on two Primus stoves and a haybox I made from an old seaman's chest. It took two saucepans. A pudding could be brought to the boil, cooked thoroughly for 20 minutes and then shoved into the haybox. Porridge could be made overnight in this way.

At the end of May 1946, my friend Mrs Mack was horrified to hear that, while I was still cooking in these primitive conditions, Ted had invited guests to stay from the British Mycological Society. So she gave me a lovely Florence stove, which included a double-skinned bread oven. You could make cakes on it, bake bread, boil water for washing up. It was super.

When we came into this house, by the way, there was also a machine which made gas – for lighting. All through the house, there were iron pipes which must have been an inch thick, with gas jets which could be lit. The machine had been out of action during the war because it had to be filled with the highest grade of petrol – aviation fuel – and the Cockles hadn't been able to get any.

When it was working, the fumes from this fuel were bubbled through water, and what remained after this process could still be used to run a car.

We didn't have a car and – in any case – petrol was still rationed. So we went over to paraffin lighting. It's a good job we did because, when we eventually took the pipes out, in 1966, we found they were rusted through. When one thinks what a blazing inferno the house might have been, I can only say it was a mercy that we couldn't get the petrol!

Later, we obtained a tiny electricity generator (hard to come by in those days) with a little engine and two large

12-and-a-half volt batteries... just enough for one, or perhaps two, 25 volt bulbs when the engine wasn't running. So at six every morning, I used to turn on one light, then dash out and pull the cord to start the engine so we could have lights while we got up and had breakfast. Then, of course, you stopped the engine until the next night.

In one sense, it was lonely. Ted was away from here at eight, and didn't get back until six. And, the village inhabitants were quite different – most were working on the land then, and the Ellises were considered... a bit strange. It was known that Ted wrote in the papers, and his name came out in relation to various meetings and committees. There was a lot of suspicion. (Russell – who would play a big part in our lives – had been warned by his brother, Aubrey, not to have anything to do with 'those strange people at Wheatfen'.)

And, you see, mothers didn't meet at the school gate in those days. Older children took younger ones to school. With water from a well, no drains and no electricity... women just didn't have the time.

Mrs Cockle, the captain's widow, moved to Margate after he died and Russell went down with her to get her house ready, get her garden in order and move her furniture. After about a month, he came back to the village but for a long time he wouldn't even cycle past this house. He missed the Cockles, of course, and was very edgy about us. I don't think he trusted us. I remember he said to me once: "I suppose you'll get rid of the bracken?" I said: "Whatever for?" and I think that began to reassure him.

Gradually, he came back and started helping us to saw wood for the fires, and helping dig the garden on Saturday afternoon or Sunday. Then he started having a cup of tea with us. Then some evenings – it happened very gradually – he would come around, and he and Ted would take a punt out. If you look at Ted's articles for 1947, it is quite surprising how often he says: "A friend and I went out on a punt ..." or something similar.

By 1948, we had some friends – the Cottons, who lived at the rectory. Kenneth was an inspector for the River Board. Then there were the Sheppards, who came here in 1947. We looked after each other's children, and went on picnics but – you see – they weren't village people.

I think I was rather tough with my children. I mean, they had this wonderful place to grow up in and a lot of freedom once they had done their chores, but I think they would tell you I was quite strict. I had to be. I had so much to do that there had to be discipline.

They were all brought up to be independent. There was John, at seven years old, when we had our first lot of Oxford students here – about 30. I remember sending John with a gallon of cocoa in one hand and a basket of cups. He had to go down to the ford, pull the boat across on the rope, get in the boat, get himself across with the rope, get out with all these things, and walk through the Decoy, taking this cocoa... all by himself.

They were brought up to help on the marshes and help in the house, and they were very helpful. Martin, aged three, could – sort of – dish out plates and ask people if they'd like a scone, and get in wood for the fire. John was always good with a boat.

They had to be independent – and remember, this place was dangerous. They had all, in their turn, fallen into the ditch – which had taught them that water is to be taken seriously. I did have the yard blocked in with gates so that they were safe, as long as nobody left the front door open. But there were times when I was worried – particularly when Mary used to put herself to bed, which she did sometimes. Then I used to rush down to the dykes, looking for her, and usually search everywhere before I thought of looking upstairs! Yes, it was worrying.

I remember Martin getting lost in the reed beds. He was three, and he screamed and screamed. And I prayed that he wouldn't get too tired and stop screaming... because the reeds were taller than he was, and it was only by the noise that I could find out where he was.

Ted began his radio career, I suppose, in 1947, when they did a programme here. By now, Russell was coming every day to help.

That summer, the two of us had a lovely holiday in Guernsey. Ted's mother and old Ethel, who had been the maid to Ted's great-aunts, came to Wheatfen to look after the children. We hadn't been to Guernsey since 1938 and, of course, we heard the most terrible tales of what it had been like during the German occupation. They had had Polish prisoners there, and treated them incredibly badly. They starved them and then, if they were found pinching a turnip, took them out and shot them.

I never forgot those stories.

The Germans had kept the dairy farms going, but the farmers had to report exactly how much milk they produced. All the milk had to go to the Germans. Bert's daughter, at the farm, was pregnant when the invasion began. She had a boy, and had to give him milk. So every morning, Bert used to get up at 2am and draw a little off one or two of his cows secretly. There was only one open side to the square of farm buildings in which the cowshed stood. He rigged a line across that side, and attached his dog on a long lead – so it would bark, and he would know if anyone was creeping about, spying on him. One morning, he came down and found the dog's body. It had had its head and tail cut off. That was the sort of thing... cruelty for cruelty's sake.

Back at home, Ted was always quite likely to bring home someone from the museum unexpectedly... a Dutchman one night, or another, I remember a German with the most wonderful embroidered linen nightshirts decorated with cross-stitching. There was an Italian another time who was, then, the only person in Italy trying to protect birds. Then there was a vegetarian Sikh who slept in a tent and ate dried bananas.

So we always had visitors. After the first few months, barely a week went by without somebody staying. Later on, we had parties for the BBC.

And apart from human visitors, of course, there were other guests...

We have always lived with hornets. Once, they had a nest in the bathroom, and if you were having a bath during the day, it was best to leave the door open so as not to confuse them as they flew backwards and forwards through the room. More recently, hornets have been nesting in the roof, and seem to get into the guests' bedroom. So we have supplied guests with a butterfly net to catch them and put them out the window. Of course, they still come in again.

Ted often rescued animals. We had storm petrels in the bath at one time... and I said 'no more petrels because they were fed on herrings. Before you had a bath, you had to clean it and the place stank of fish. We had a gull which I was rather frightened of, and a heron with a broken leg which was terrifying. They go for the eyes. Very fierce.

With all the music in my family, it is no wonder that the children were brought up with music. I started John and Mary on the piano at a very early age: "A, A shows the way. Let us play another A... Here is B, as you see, just above the A, you see. A, B .. A. B, A ... B. AB, AB. Next comes C." But, of course, I had babies to look after, wood fires to keep alight... and, like all children, they found practising a nuisance. But, in the end, they all played one instrument or another.

I started going to Surlingham church soon after we moved here. We didn't have a proper parson, but one of the history masters from the grammar school came out on a Sunday for an evening service. I would put Mary and Martin to bed, and Ted stayed behind to look after them. Then I used to ride up to the church on Ted's bicycle, with John on the seat in front.

They ran out of organists in the winter of 1946, so I was asked to play and – yes – John, just about five, did actually pump the organ for me... as well as helping to saw up wood at home.

I played the organ at the church until 1948. Then I was expecting Lucy in early August. So in July I had to refuse to go any more... in case I suddenly had the baby, on the spot! One expected to have the fourth one quite quickly.

In July of that year, we hired a wooden hut on Scolt Head Island for a week. I was worried. I had been unwell. For once, my legs swelled. I already had three children and Ted was far from well too though he wouldn't admit it. I remember a filthy storm one night, about the last night before we were due to leave the island. I thought I was going into labour. I had all these peculiar pains, and the thunder and lightning was going on. Ted wrote an article about it:

FOAM AND SAND-DRIFT

Scolt Head Island, July 5th 1948

'Yesterday evening, the last ragged fringes of the rain curtain vanished and for a moment the sun appeared to glorify the sea with a trail of fire.

Then came an ominous calm below, while three distinct layers of clouds were agitated by criss-cross currents in the heavens. The wind shifted to the north-west and freshened quickly to a gale, which smote us furiously all through the grey night. This morning, the white horses were flying towards the beach and great walls of foam were quivering and spilling over the tidemark.

Much of the foam, concentrated to a sort of half-melted sticky essence as its iridescent bubbles subsided, became resolved into grey-brown scum, revealing the presence of fine mud carried hither from the Wash, as well as bilge oil and other less tangible flotsam.

When the wind freed lumps of this stuff, they went bowling along, picking up an increasing crust of mud and beach sand until the accumulation of an extreme load proved their undoing; their progress was marked by groove-like tracks, so that the beach came to look as though it had been combed with a rake.

*Tons of sand were being swept from the shore into the shelter of
the marram hills. The finer particles made a blizzard mist
whisked high into the air, while larger grit and fragments of
shell could be seen trickling up slopes and shuffling around
obstructions like grain being jiffled out of a threshing machine.*

*The sharp flinty leaves of the marram grass went into action in a
curious way; as the wind blew off and on they cut semicircular
grooves in the sand so that the hillocks on which they grew
became fortified with a series of holes and ditches, like ancient
earthworks.'*

Lucy was born on August 17 in the big, wooden bedroom
upstairs. I was shrieking blue murder. She was upside down
and had one leg stuck. It was an awful muddle. I had phoned
the nurse about seven in the morning, but she had been
out, delivering twins up the road. When she finally arrived,
she was tired and – perhaps not thinking clearly – wouldn't
send for the doctor.

In the end, Ted fetched the doctor, who was extremely cross.
He quickly put me under, and got the child out. She never
would have come out. She'd got one leg doubled up under
her chin.

We didn't have our own car until 1949, but in 1947 Ted's
brother, Martin, had been married and had moved into a
flat in London with his wife, Pam, who had been an Army
driver and mechanic. In London, they had nowhere safe
to keep her car... so it was 'stabled' at Wheatfen. It was a
1934 Triumph, the last of the tiny Triumphs, a beautiful
little car with an aluminium body and real leather seats.
If you could get it to go at 50mph, you were travelling
indeed! They let us use it, and Ted – who had been travelling

to work, at first by bicycle and later on a moped – passed his driving test in 1948.

At the beginning of 1949, Mary went to school. She was four-and-a-half. Then, in June, Ted finally had a haemorrhage. From 1948, it had been obvious this illness was coming, but he always told people to mind their own business. He was down to seven stone and, after all, he was 5ft 10in… but he still told people to mind their own business.

The last straw had been when, although he was ill, he cut a path through the reed for a visiting party of botanists. It must have been the best part of half a mile. I was absolutely furious because, even when he had the haemorrhage, he never told me. He just got someone to take him to the doctor in Blofield – after all the years of my telling him he ought to go. The doctor ordered him home and straight to bed.

It was June 17. The rhododendrons were late flowering that year, and there were still a few pheasant's eye narcissi about. I moved the bed round so that he could see out of the bay window.

From that September until the end of January 1950, he was in hospital at Kelling. That was a hard time – trying to visit Ted, looking after four small children. Lucy was just over a year, and also unwell. Then there was Martin, three-and-three-quarters, Mary aged five and John, eight.

We had a fairly good bus service in those days. Visiting times were Wednesday, Saturday and Sunday. I could get a bus from Surlingham into the city or cycle and, from there, buses went out on Saturday and Sunday. Wednesdays, I had to beg a lift.

I started having driving lessons – so I could drive to Kelling to visit Ted if Uncle Frank or my father were beside me. But I don't think I told Ted that. He would have had fits!

Then we had trouble with the springs on the car which – being a 1934 car – were coach springs underneath the seats. Mr Braybrook, who had the garage and was working on it, had a heart attack. So he was sent to bed, and the car was left in bits all over the garage floor. Fortunately, Uncle Frank was staying. He was very clever, and had worked for Fords in America. But he had a bad heart, too, and must have been over 60.

So I was the one who had to crawl under the car and put it back together, trying to follow Uncle Frank's instructions, with layers of clothes on (because it was December, in a bitterly cold garage). Periodically, when we weren't sure which bits came next, we'd go upstairs and talk to Mr Braybrook in his sick bed.

I've certainly done some funny jobs! Anyhow, the car worked. So the hospital visits continued.

During this time, I didn't just have the children at home. Old Ethel always came for a month at Christmas. When she wasn't there, my father came or Uncle Frank. Sometimes Ted's mother came.

It meant I always had someone to look after the children. But, on the other hand, it was a worry. Ted's mother couldn't cope with stairs very well. Frank had a very bad heart. My father had a dicky heart, too.

I looked around at all these candles and paraffin lamps and open fires one day, and thought: "What am I doing? If we suddenly had a fire, who would I rescue first? The old people or the children?"

By this stage, Russell was spending all his free time here, but working for his brother and living with his sister and two brothers at No 1 Brickyard – now called Brickyard Farm. We spoke about it one evening, and he said: "If you can find me a room, I'll gladly sleep here at nights." We had a loggia with two bunks for guests. And that was how we arranged it.

Ted came home from Kelling on January 31st 1950. He still weighed only seven stone, and was fairly touchy, to say the least. He'd had a bad time, and I understood that. But it didn't mean, because I understood, that I would put up with it. Breakfast times used to be... a little difficult.

He wasn't best pleased to find me driving, either. I was always 'too near the edge of the road' or 'too near the middle of the road' or it was "Mind that cyclist!". The final straw came when the gear stick broke off in my hand. Of course, that was 'my fault', too. So I gave up, and didn't drive again until 1965. I obviously wasn't going to drive with him in the car!

Altogether, Ted was off work for 14 months. After six months on full pay, and six months on half pay, we followed up with two months on no pay. By the beginning of 1951, it was obvious we hadn't got anything left in the bank, so I went back to teaching. Rockland School had been ringing me. They needed someone to take the infants. I'd turned them down before – because one of the children was always ill and Lucy, especially, was ill, off and on, until she was seven.

But that January, I did go back to Rockland School, where I had been in 1942. I went back 'temporarily' I thought, though it turned out to be for 21 years!

When I went back into teaching, I could quite easily have got a headship. I had done several locum headships during the war and – with a London training – it wouldn't have been difficult. I wouldn't have gone into town to teach, not for anything. I liked Rockland School. And besides, if you are Head, you have to devote your time to being Head. You can't suddenly say: "One of my children is ill. I can't come in this morning." So I turned it down, when – later – it was offered.

Anyhow, Lucy was two-and-a-half but we were able to send her to a nanny at Claxton. Mary and John were at school. Martin was four, not really old enough, but I took him with me and he thoroughly enjoyed going into the infants' class.

Come September, Martin was old enough to go to Claxton School. Russell took him on his bicycle until Martin was old enough to walk. It was one-and-a-half miles across the fields, and Martin walked it in all weathers after he was about six. Well, I suppose I didn't think anything of it because, from three-and-a-half, I'd been used to walking a long way to school myself. You couldn't do it nowadays.

But all this was necessary, you see. The money I earned really kept the household going. I enjoyed my years with the infants, but it wasn't my idea of looking after a family ... that you put your own children out for somebody else to look after.

Rockland had pail closets which were emptied regularly, so it was comparatively modern. But at Surlingham, to my horror, they were still using privies. Old Palmer, who lived opposite, took a scoop and emptied them once a week, for which he was paid 10 shillings – as much, practically, as the old age pension in those days.

Anyhow, I got up at the end of the annual general parish meeting, and said I thought it was an absolute disgrace that they still had privies in 1951. Well, the difference in attitude between then and now... about a WOMAN getting up in PUBLIC and talking about CLOSETS (I think I called it a 'shit house', actually) at the GENERAL MEETING when MEN WERE PRESENT! The whole audience was shocked. There was a definite feeling that 'Mrs Ellis wasn't really fit to know'. (You know, 'Those Ellises... very strange people!')

I told them that if the parish council couldn't do anything about it, and the education committee couldn't do anything about it, I would write to my MP.

Children's parties and children's picnics were a part of the pattern of our lives and a particularly happy part of the pattern. Mary's class would come out and we'd go swimming in the ford. Once I started teaching again, children would come from Rockland and play in the woods. Like my grandfather, you see, I always wanted to bring outside things into school... and bring school into outside things.

Once we had a connection to the High School, they liked to bring children on excursions... so we had groups ranging from infants to fifth or sixth formers doing projects.

As our children grew older, they continued to bring their friends here... happy times! Though I do remember Mary, aged 10, and her friends once tied Martin to a tree, and left him there... and forgot about him! He was tied to that

tree all day. I never missed him, not even at meal times...
which shows what sort of parent I was!

I remember in 1951, our first proper children's party. John
was at Bracondale School, so there were boys from
Bracondale and girls from the High School. We didn't have
much money, but I got balls of wool and wound them up
the stairs, over beds, under tables and down the back stairs,
and I tied on packets of Smarties and various things. So you
had each child winding up their wool, and getting muddled
up and in a tangle... it took quite a while!

Another thing was to hide dried peas... on top of skirtings,
in corners, everywhere. You gave each child a cup, to see
how many they could gather.

On other occasions, the children would go swimming.
From 1947 until 1953, the water here was pure and clear.
It suddenly altered in 1953, with the advent of new
detergents and swimming had to end. The weeds died,
and the water became murky.

At Christmas, we usually had people staying. Then we
played games... and that was when we started with charades.
I used to keep a dressing-up chest, an extraordinary chest
with a whole lot of rubbish... scarves and so on.

Then half the people went out of the room, and somebody
put on a performance – like miming to buy a ticket on a
bus. One by one, the people came back in, and watched
and each had to repeat the performance for the next
person to come back in... until the last one had to guess
what it was supposed to be. Of course, by then it had got
gradually transmuted...

And so the evening passed. We always finished by singing

round the piano, ending up with 'The Holy City'. That is a real tradition of the family, that you end any sort of party with 'The Holy City'. You remember them, because the parties were all different.

Our Christmases could be quite an eye-opener, as you can imagine, for our various guests – such as, on one occasion, a French girl and a Japanese professor. Perhaps they got a rather funny idea of the English.

Later, in the 1960s, we began to hire the village hall. Then we had parties for children and parents... and grandparents, with a lot of games. People would have a name stuck on their back and would have to guess who they were by going around, asking other people questions. There was dancing on a newspaper... and you and your partner had to tear it in half and stand on it each time the music stopped.

We usually did a play on the platform. One year, we did Roald Dahl's Snow White and the Seven Dwarfs. By this time, the children were grown up... so we had Martin, 6ft 6in, as a dwarf (on his knees). I was a dwarf too!

And then, it would be midnight and time to go home.

It all gets very uproarious. Our parties have always been rather riotous affairs – old fashioned, the sort of parties the Irish have at a wake. Perhaps there's still enough Irish blood in me, five centuries away.

In the later 1940s, Russell and I were still sawing fallen trunks for fuel – sawing them into six-foot lengths then splitting them with wedges, bringing them home in a three-wheeled trolley that we could drag across the marshes.

Then about 1950, we eventually bought a huge, old-fashioned generator with a 1912 Lister engine. We needed a lorry to bring it home. It had a lot of glass batteries. I think there were 26, and each was two volts. This meant we could run a pump for water as well as lighting the house. The engine could also run a circular saw, and help to cut the wood – which was marvellous. Unfortunately, it only lasted for about a year... then it was back to Tilley lamps.

Of course, there are disadvantages to everything. That year, the hornets built a nest in the garage as big as a two-gallon pail. As we sawed, they would be flying down and picking the sawdust out of the air to take back and go on building their nest.

After the 1953 floods, Ken Cotton, the River Board engineer and our great friend, asked Ted what he should plant to stabilise the Cley shingle bank. Ted recommended Sea Pea, and we all went down with pillowslips in late August. We all sat on the beach getting Sea Pea seeds, which we brought back and sowed all over the shingle bank.

We had a marvellous crop there for a few years – just long enough to get other plants established. There are still a few around the east end.

I was highly pregnant at this time. Suzie was born in that November.

The day Suzie was born, I'd realised I was going to have the baby, and I got up in the middle of the night, shifted one of the children – asleep – on to another bed, took the old iron bedstead to bits, and brought it downstairs because I thought, with four children already, I'd better be handy.

Chapter Eleven

So I made the bed, and phoned the nurse about seven in the morning. Everything was an awful muddle. Russell had taken our Rayburn stove to bits, and couldn't get the new firebricks in. The doctor was living in Brundall, so Ted had to go and fetch him across by ferry.

By now it was mid-morning, and I was in the middle of labour pains... and making a bit of a fuss. I was never one to take birth quietly. At this point, Martin was brought in from school with a terrible wound on his leg, right down to the bone. The poor teacher who had brought him back was horrified to find the whole house in uproar, people bustling around for hot water, and me screaming my head off!

She dumped him and ran!

Fortunately, the doctor was there by that time, and saw to Martin and his wound.

Despite the fuss, as soon as I had had Suzie, I sat up in bed, all smiles, wanting a cup of tea and I was alright. I never had any depression after childbirth. I'd got it out of my system.

Anyhow, I went back to school at Easter 1954, when Suzie was four months old. I had Mrs Bury to help me by looking after Suzie.

By 1956 – the year John joined the Navy, as an apprentice – Ted had decided to give up museum work, finish writing his Broads book and then earn his keep through writing. He wrote for various publications – a fishing magazine, a church publication and the EDP and later on The Guardian. But the money just wasn't there, so I continued teaching – still not expecting it to be indefinitely.

Edna Coe came to help in the mornings, with housework. In fact, Edna wasn't very happy about coming here, at first. There had been a piece in the paper about Ted being president of the Norfolk Naturalists Trust and, unfortunately, the Eastern Daily Press had reported it as the 'Naturists Trust'. No wonder!

Added, to that, I remember one pouring wet day in holiday time, when John was about six, Mary, three and Martin on his feet at 18 months, the children had wanted to go outside. It had been a warm summer's day, so I said "OK, you can take your clothes off and go outside naked". They had a lovely time, playing under dripping gutters and rushing around with tins of water. Well, it never struck me at the time, but the men had been working on the field nearby, and I'm sure the story was taken home that the children were running around naked.

So – as I learned later – Edna was very worried during the first few months she was with me in case Ted suddenly started taking his clothes off!

Edna was very good to my father – who was living here by this time. After he retired, my father had lived at St Olave's on his own, for a long time, in the bungalow we had used when I was a child. But he came to live with us at about this time, and had a small caravan in the woods, where he slept.

Russell used to light Father's fire every morning, before he went to work. Father made his own breakfast, and came in to have lunch here.

When Ted came home from Kelling, Russell had stopped sleeping here, though he used to come around every evening and sit with us, and chat to Ted or read the dictionary –

one of his favourite books. However, one night – it might have been a couple of years after Ted returned from Kelling, a terrible gale had got up and trees were falling down in the lane. Ted said he'd better stay that night, and not risk going home. After that, he always slept here.

So every morning at 7am, before Russell went off to work, he stood at the well with a bucket on a string, and passed the water in through the kitchen window to me, while I rushed to pour it into containers – a big bath and a tank from a water purifier. Then Russell left for work at 7.30am and I left, on a bicycle, at 8am. And this went on for years. As we got a bigger family... we had to get more water in!

Note from family: At this time, Phyllis employed Freda Hayhow who became our absolute rock over the next 30 or so years. She arrived on her bike from Rockland before Phyllis left for work and stayed until she returned. Freda cheerfully looked after Ted and any sick children, did household chores, coped with the piles of dirty gumboots and the Ellis muddle and kept us all in order with her dry humour and affection. Phyllis continued to do all the cooking, usually on a large scale, as there were so many of us in the house.

Ted did need looking after, in various ways.

He was always bringing people home, for example – to be fed, and perhaps to stay the night. I remember one particular visitor who liked to sit and talk until four in the morning, and started coming here regularly. Well, Ted had been ill – and needed his sleep – and teaching is quite exhausting. So I started, when he was coming, only half-filling the Tilley lamps so that about 10pm they started wavering and going out. And I didn't make the fire up after 8pm. So by about 10 or 10.30, the fire would be dying down to red ash, and

we would look at it and say: "Oh well, the fire's going...
the light is going... we might as well go to bed."

On another occasion, Ted was due to give an important
talk in the afternoon, and I met him for lunch at the BBC.
It must have been a school holiday... Anyway, he could
never drink much without it showing. A pint and a half
was enough to make him garrulous, and you know what
people are like in pubs. We went across to the Surrey Street
pub for a drink after lunch, and he had a half pint. Then
somebody said: "Have another?"

Ted said "No, thank you" but the man signed to the barman,
who filled it up and passed it across, and they said: "Well,
you've got it now anyway."

So I said: "Oh no he hasn't!" and tipped it up and drank it
myself. I said: "He's not having it because he's giving a talk.
He already told you he didn't want it, and you needn't have
ordered it", and I marched out of that pub – followed by
Ted, who was deeply ashamed of me, no doubt. But it was
necessary. It had to be done.

I've never been back to that pub since.

I used to get frustrated because he would never push himself
forward. One time, he gave a talk at Wolferton WI after
Christmas – when the Queen and Queen Mother always
attended. It was a lovely talk. Ted had really gone to town
to find his best slides. The Queen said: "I wish Philip was
here." And, you see, if it had been me, I would have said:
"Would you like me to come to Sandringham?" But Ted
would never do that. And I couldn't very well shout out
from the back! Ted was his own man, and what he said went.

I must say, earlier on that same evening, Ted had put his screen up in front of the stage and set up his projector, but the people arranging the chairs were so anxious that the Queen should be in the front that they put her in front of the projector. I said to the president: "I'm awfully sorry, but you'll have to get them to move their chairs."

Consternation!

She said: "Oh! I can't do that!" So I said: "Well, I suppose I'll have to, then." It was me who had to go up and say: "Excuse me, Ma'am, but if Ted is going to use the projector... can I move your chair for you?" I mean, it was ridiculous ... nobody could go and ask them!

***

After he left the museum, Ted started to do more wireless work. He had a programme on the Midland Home Service (now Radio 4) called Nature Postbag. Once he had been on the radio two or three times, he began to be known and we began to have people ringing up. You'd just be sitting down for a meal, and someone would be phoning up asking what to do about a sparrow that had fallen out of its nest. So I learned a certain amount of... what I call rough-and-ready answers to common natural history questions, having heard him talking about it, and if he wasn't about (or didn't hear the phone ring), I often answered them myself, and didn't call him. Or I would ask people to call back in an hour. That would help.

He got very cross when he found me doing that, but I didn't see me cooking a good meal – which he needed –

and then trying to keep it warm while he chatted on the phone for 20 minutes. I did get the reputation of being rather a dragon, and over-protecting him. But it needed to be done.

That was the only protection I could give him. I was not allowed to help him very much. I did suggest answering letters for him – if he just jotted down a few lines. But he preferred to do it himself.

In fact, visitors who came to the house quite often didn't even realise he was married. I would answer the door, and they would say: "Is Mr Ellis in?" and be rather surprised when I shouted up the stairs: "Ted!" They were even more surprised to find he had five children. I don't think he talked about his family very much, outside of the house.

I did insist that we had a proper holiday as often as we could afford it. That was one thing I could do.

In 1957, Ted's mother came here, a lovely woman – one of the kindest people I have ever known. Ted's father had died when Lucy was two, and his mother had lived alone for some time. She was with us for the last... nearly a year. She died in March 1958.

Ted's mother was very deaf. Then there was Mrs Gorballs, a friend of my father, who sometimes came to stay for a week and was very, very, VERY deaf. The two of them would be in the sitting room, and one would say: "It's raining outside." And the other would say: "Yes, I do like knitting." And they would carry on that way for the week!

For the last six weeks, Ted's mother had a palliasse on the floor, downstairs. I used to sleep on the floor beside her.

This was February. We kept a big fire going all night. She would sleep for a couple of hours, then want to get up. I'd get up at six, make tea and get the children up. In the evening, Mary or Martin would sit with her while they did their homework. Then I'd go to bed at seven and Ted would take over. He would wake me at 10, and go to bed himself. That was how we managed. Ted had been ill, you see.

Anyhow, Ted's mother retained her mind until the very end. She had been a Roman Catholic, and one of her brothers wrote to the Catholic Church in Norwich, saying he would like her to receive the Last Rites. So I was rung up, and asked if I would mind a priest calling.

I said I didn't mind but warned them that Mother had not been a Catholic since before 1900, when her first husband died. Whether she would want the Last Rites, I couldn't say.

Well, this young priest arrived on a white motorbike, with a white helmet and a white motorcycle jacket. He wanted a little table and a cloth. So I found that. Mother was in her armchair, so I went out to the kitchen.

Five minutes later, he tore out of the room, scarlet in the face, dashed out of the door, where he collided with the coalman, and departed without saying goodbye. When I went back in, she was laughing, saying: "I did 'im, I did 'im." What she said to him, I never found out. She would never tell me, and she died about midnight. It was very gentle.

My father was 78 when he died, in 1962.

His caravan in the woods – where he had lived for the last seven years – had been his 'nest', so to speak, with an all-purpose stove. When he was tired, in the afternoons, he'd go back there, find a service on the radio and lie on his bed playing along to the hymn tunes on his ocarina. He no longer played the banjo, and I think at some point he must have given it to Martin.

He used to potter about, and he had his boat moored at the bottom of the dyke. Every day he went up to Coldham Hall for his pint of beer, and once a week took his three-wheeler, a Morgan, to visit an old friend at Cobham.

It was shortly after Ted's mother died that Father had his first stroke. He'd had it in the caravan. He didn't turn up for his cup of tea in the afternoon, and we had gone across and found him on the bed. We decided it was time he left the caravan. The room where Ted's mother died now became his bedroom.

In fact, he recovered fantastically quickly. One of his hands was affected, but the next day he was writing a letter. But over a period, he had another five or six slight strokes. At this time, he still went out on his boat, but he had changed his sailing boat for a Victorian-type launch – mahogany, quite long, with a wheel to steer in the middle.

Now, he had been used to a rudder, you see, and when you want to go right, you steer the opposite way. He used to go out on it by himself, steer the wrong way and land up on the bank. Once, he came down the Fen Channel from Rockland Broad, and got stuck in a glyceria bed, just the other side of Deep Waters. It was an absolute swamp. He couldn't walk to the shore, and he couldn't make anybody hear that he was there and in trouble.

Do you know how he got home? He'd got two oars. So he

got an oar out and laid it on the mud, and crawled from where the boat was to the path on his stomach with the oar.

Ted was very annoyed, and said: "You mustn't let him go out in the boat like that by himself." But I was working full-time, playing organ on Sundays, on Saturday doing the cooking for the week... in the end, I phoned the doctor, and said: "What am I to do with my father? He keeps stranding the boat, but he's so happy."

The doctor said: "Leave him alone. He's happy. He's 78. When you're old like that, it's much better to keep doing the thing you like doing. If there's an accident, well... it can't be helped."

It wasn't long after that that he had his sixth stroke. This time, it was all down his right side. And he couldn't move. The doctor said: "If you like, we'll send him to Whitlingham Hospital." But I could see the old man was listening, and he'd got his eye on my mother's ashes, which he kept in an urn on the mantlepiece, and polished every week. So I said: "It's alright, we'll look after him here."

After all, there were enough of us.

I slept in the hall, nearby, on a mattress with the door open. Russell and I would get him up. A male nurse came to wash him. This went on for six weeks. Eventually, pneumonia set in and he died quickly – and quite conveniently – just after I'd given the children breakfast. We just shut the door, and then attended to what had to be done after the children had gone to school.

About the time Ted's mother died, I was looking for a little box for some reason, and I went into Ted's den, thinking he must have one somewhere. I found a very nice one, covered in purple with a lid – just what I wanted. But when I opened it, I found lots of little bits of white, like snail shells and thought: "What the devil are these?"

It was the Old Man's ashes – Ted's father – that he'd brought home from the crematorium, stuck on the shelf and apparently forgotten!

So when his mother was buried, I put that box in the coffin with her. Then, later, when my father died, his ashes went into the urn with my mother's, and the parson very kindly came with us while we opened the grave and put the urn in with Ted's parents. It was very naughty of us. I don't suppose there's any proper record. But all four parents are in the same unmarked grave at Surlingham churchyard.

Mary left home, to go to Durham, in 1962, the year my father died. I was losing them all, one by one. Martin was about to leave a year after Mary in 1963... with, as it happened, quite a send-off.

At that time, I was making birch wine, blackberry wine... all sorts. I also brewed beer. The BBC sometimes liked to come and have a bonfire in the woods, and a barbecue. Now, for this particular BBC party I had really put my back into it, and brewed some good, strong beer.

It wasn't all drunk... Martin was 18, and leaving school a couple of weeks later, and wanted a party, so I let them have the rest of the beer – not realising it had got even stronger. They had a bonfire and sausages – but after a while I could hear all this noise, like a football field, and there were all these boys running through the woods, swinging on trees and across the marshes, and I realised I couldn't send them home like that.

One boy had his father's car. We kept him till about three in the morning, on strong coffee, walking him round. One had cycled from Wymondham, and he was the parson's son. I had to ring up his father and say he wasn't well... and would have to stay the night. I'm sure he didn't believe me.

One boy's father had a taxi, so he collected several of the others – and delivered them home somewhere after midnight. Oh dear! That taught me!

John, of course, had been the first to leave home – going into the Navy as an engineer apprentice before he was 16. He passed his first exams brilliantly, and was sent up to Scotland, where we went to his passing-out parade.

Mary went to Durham to study French with Spanish as a subsidiary. Then Martin went to Newcastle to do Botany with Genetics. Lucy, in her turn, went to Yarmouth Art School just before she was 18 to take a pre-diploma course, then to Wolverhampton to take a degree in ceramics. Suzie went to Sheffield and studied Art.

Willy, who came to live with us when he was 12, about 1960, had first visited with a group from a private boarding school. Then he came for a weekend, and seemed to settle in with my lot – and eventually came to live here. He was an intelligent child – clever with his hands. He joined the Army and was later apprenticed, in Germany, to make viols.

I retired from teaching in 1973, by which time I was 60. Ted was in a better position financially and, of course, we had fewer children at college living on grants. Since I was over 40 when I had Suzie, by the time I retired, she was only 20 and still at art school in Sheffield. So, in a sense, we still had young people around.

Ted with an injured heron in the hallway at Wheatfen

Ted, Russell and Mr Sharman, a reedcutter, circa 1957?

Jack Chambers in his boat at Wheatfen 1960

Willy Bailey and a harpsichord he made circa 1970

John with Alice and Jimmy Ellis 1944

Doris Carr and Freda Hayhow in 1984

Ted and Phyllis 1985 Ted's hat was made by Phyllis from coypu fur she had cured herself.

Phyllis outside Buckingham Palace 1996 after receiving her MBE with Colin, Mary, Lucy, Phyllis, Anne, Martin and Suzie

Chapter Twelve

"He came home and had the most wonderful fortnight"

A PASSING ON

Ted's BBC television programme – with John Mountford – had run for a considerable time. They had a million listeners, and received up to 90 letters a week – which Ted insisted on answering personally. Then in July 1985, they had a new producer and the programme was ended. They weren't needed any more.

From that time, Ted altered. He continued with his *In The Countryside* articles for the EDP, his *Nature's Byways* and his fishing articles, but his health went down. Just before Christmas, we tried to persuade him to go to a doctor but he wouldn't go.

In the following May, we went to a friend's 80th birthday, and a photograph was taken of Ted talking to the gardener. When the picture came home, I was really shocked by what he looked like – because, of course, when you live with someone you perhaps don't notice how they are going down until you are confronted with something like a photograph.

In fact, he had made the birthday speech, and it had been very amusing and everybody had thought, you know, how cheerful he was and so on... he could always put on a good show, but I was the one who had to drive there and back. He couldn't drive any more. I'd seen how tired he was, and I remember I thought then: "This is it."

In June, the Norfolk Naturalists' Trust had a big day on the marshes at Cley, and he was down to take two walks right along the shingle bank – quite a long way. It was terribly cold and, by this time, he was on bread and milk. He had really stopped eating. So he took the first walk, then came back to the car – and he was absolutely whacked.

A week later, he was in hospital. Anyhow, he had an operation. He was in hospital quite a time, but he had masses of visitors. All the hospital staff used to come to see him, all the doctors and consultants. He was very popular.

He came home, and had the most wonderful fortnight. The sun shone and he sat outside, and tottered up the marsh as far as the machan, or up the wood as far as the campfire site – all the time still writing articles. Again, he had masses of visitors. There was laughing and talking, but he wasn't getting better...

Eventually, I ordered an ambulance. Ted went out in his slippers and dressing gown. He walked out. And that was it, you see. That must have been the Thursday.

When we went down to the hospital, I went in and I was sitting there. We were really being rather silent. I hadn't got much to say and he was obviously dying. And he turned around and said: "You know, we never did much together, did we, not even when we had retired?"

I said: "Oh, we had some nice holidays... Guernsey and so on."

But in a sense we did lead separate lives. We didn't chat very much. I produced meals at the right time... After I retired from teaching in 1972, we could have done more.

But if I said "wouldn't it be nice if we went to so-and-so", he'd often say "Oh, I'm waiting for a call from the BBC" or "I want to do something in my den".

Of course, when I was teaching I suppose I spent more time thinking about my school-children and their needs than – perhaps my own family. It's very difficult when you've got a job that you are extremely interested in, and you enjoy.

He died on the Monday. We went down to the hospital, and he was just lying there. I suppose he was unconscious. He didn't react when I spoke to him, but it was extraordinary... You could see all these thoughts going around in his head, masses of ideas and memories. I wish I could have known what he was thinking. I stayed until about 10am, then they came to remake the bed. So I went down to the bank, to put a cheque in that he'd signed for me the previous week. I came back, and I suppose he passed away about an hour later.

It was all very gentle. So were all the deaths. I had two die here, my father and my mother-in-law. Two died in hospital – Russell and Ted. They weren't upsetting. All the deaths were very gentle.

Lucy came up. She was in time to see him before they took him away. We just sat in the public room, where everybody waits. And I thought – well, it was alright because death, to me, is only a passing on.

Phyllis and David Bellamy 1995

Reproduced with kind permission of Anglia Television

Chapter Thirteen

"The value of Wheatfen lies not just in what we already know but in what we haven't yet found"

AFTER TED

I played the organ at his funeral. I wasn't going to sit in the front seat. It was a celebratory occasion, with a lot of lovely music. We had the 15th psalm, which I have always thought was very much like Ted – "the man who had no deceit on his tongue".

Anyhow, after he died, we had very little money. By the time I'd paid for his funeral, the bank account was empty. You see, Ted had never demanded his true worth in money. He should have had an agent, but you couldn't persuade him. ("Oh, they'll pay me what I'm worth," he always said.) So the end of the month was always a hard time, even after I went back to teaching.

I had a state pension, and a small teaching pension. I could afford to go on living at Wheatfen – but not to run a car. So we decided to sell some of the marshes to a Trust.

Tony Irwin from the Castle Museum was extremely helpful. We had a preliminary meeting of people I thought might be interested at the end of October, 1986. So we didn't really waste much time.

A meeting was held in early October and a committee was formed. Dr Roy Baker from the UEA and Keith Clarke from Anglian Water agreed to be trustees. A one-sheet

pamphlet was rushed out and distributed at Ted's Thanks-giving Service in Norwich Cathedral on October 31, setting out the Trust's aims.

Roy undertook fundraising. Keith and Tony drew up a management plan. David Pearce-Gould, an accountant, joined to help on the financial side and became the third trustee.

We obtained registered charity status, and enough money was raised in less than a year to buy the 102 acres of marsh-land. We also formed a group 'Friends of the Ted Ellis Trust' – for people who would actually work for the Trust, to gather money and do jobs around the place, on the marshes.

During these years, I was also a Surlingham parish councillor...

In parish politics, you need a free speaker who isn't connected to any... political society. It's a great pity, I think, when politics comes into local councils – so that people group together even if they don't think alike. I first joined the parish council about 1982. I did eight years; then I decided I had had enough.

I said: "I'll be over 80 if I do another four years." Well, after a four-year gap, so many people asked me to put my name up that I did – and came top of the poll, much to everyone's amazement, including me.

Anyhow, the first talk I gave, for the Trust, I think Ted had been dead about a year. I had never spoken publicly, except in school. Then one day, I saw an Adrian Bell article which Ted had left pinned to the wall. Adrian Bell used to write in the Press every Saturday, and this article was about how he had been putting his trousers on one morning, and Ted had come on the radio... and Adrian had paused to listen, with one leg in and one leg out.

I saw it, and thought I would like to read it on the radio. I knew that Skip – Keith Skipper – sometimes read Adrian Bell's articles on Radio Norfolk so I went to see him and explained. Skip said: "Well, I'll read it for you." but I said: "No, I want to read it myself." He wasn't keen. "Do you think you can?" But I said: "It's alright... I do know how to read", and he agreed.

You see, in the days when I trained as a teacher, we were given lectures on reading aloud. There is a certain skill to it, and it is one of the things I can do.

So I went on the radio, and I spoke about Ted, and I went on from there – reading various articles, once a fortnight and later once a month. I found some of Ted's articles and sorted them into months so I could read something connected with the weather, and what was happening now in the countryside. That went on for six years.

Now, in that first broadcast I also spoke about all the stuff Ted had left – rooms full of papers in boxes – and how I wanted to sort it all out, but didn't know how. Well, Diana Davey was in her car. Apparently it was raining, and she was waiting somewhere and happened to turn her radio on. She wrote me such a nice letter, saying: "I don't know much about natural history, but I am a pharmacist and I could come and help you if you like."

So she came to see me and, after that, came most Monday nights. Diana would arrive about seven and each week we would sit down and tackle one box. Apart from the fact

that we sometimes met with mouse dirt – not to mention
spiders – we got on remarkably quickly. We wore aprons.
Sometimes, I think we should have had face masks...
because some of the boxes were very, very old and there
was a lot of dust!

We began sorting them into ten different headings:
committee meetings, for example... BBC letters connected
with programmes... letters with specimens. I made strong
brown envelopes. One envelope was simply called 'lists',
which might have been anything written on the back of
an old envelope or a matchbox. He would use whatever
was handy when he wanted to make a note: a piece of
toilet paper or, once, a great big roll of paper that must
have come out of some sort of adding machine.

I took the sorted packets to Dr Tony Irwin at Norwich
Castle Museum. He has been wonderful, and has arranged
for people to sort slides, sort letters into subjects and years.
People were very anxious to help.

After we got rid of the boxes, his books all went up to the
museum, where they were put on a database by Dr Irwin.
The slides, *In the Countryside Notes* and *Nature's Byways*
articles have all been put on a database by Chris Blenkiron.
There was also Ted's fungi collection. I considered it should
be a local collection, and there was enough material for
the specimens to be halved – with part of it kept at the
Castle Museum in Norwich and part at the Mycological
Institute in London.

Dr Richard Dennis, an old friend who has been doing
voluntary work in mycology at Kew since he retired took
on the task of dividing and cataloguing it, and in 1996 it
was finished.

So I have had a lot of help, and made a lot of good friends through the years.

Wheatfen is an ecosystem which has not been altered for 400 years – apart from the woods, which were replanted. Research is still going on, and we are still discovering new things here. There are more than 800 species of beetles here, for example, which have now been listed, including some extremely rare ones.

The value of Wheatfen lies not just in what we already know, but in what we haven't yet found.

Wheatfen House 1919

Wheatfen after Captain Cockle's shiplap extension 1920

Wheatfen, Norfolk Naturalist's Trust outing 1970s

Chapter Fourteen

SOME HISTORY OF WHEATFEN

Our home at Wheatfen was originally a pair of marshmen's cottages. There was a stable for the horse and – where the garage is now – an open cart shed. There was a walnut tree in the yard, so they had walnuts to eat, and a good garden. One cottage had the back garden and the other, had the front garden.

The entrance was not where it is now, but up by the big beech tree, and the roadway came down to the marsh (past the end of the house opposite the kitchen) through where one of the tool huts is now, and down to the marsh that way.

They were good cottages, with a 12 foot living room and 12 foot bedroom.

I know all this, you see, because Russell Sewell was seven when he left here, in 1907. He had been born in one of the two cottages, the seventh child.

By then, his parents were already quite old. His father must have been born about 1850. At least three of the children, I suppose, would have been out to work. So perhaps the oldest son, Richard, was still living at home – but he would be at work on the fields as a labourer. The two eldest daughters, Violet and Lily, had gone out as maids. I know that Violet went to work when she was 12.

After Russell, there were two – if not three – more children born at the cottage. It was a tied house, so Russell's father didn't pay rent. When the family moved out, there were so many children that they were given two clapboard cottages. Eventually, there were 13 children.

Russell's mother was a Fuller, and they were a Rockland family going back many years. His uncle was 'Old Scientific' Fuller, about whom James Wentworth-Day wrote and whose picture is in Arthur Patterson's *'Poachers and Wildfowlers'*.

At some time, Wheatfen had been part of a shooting estate for a Lord Jackson. I am not sure how much of Wheatfen he had, and how much other land. Unfortunately, there are no records prior to Captain Cockle. The earlier deeds must have been burnt when he took it on in 1914. Lord Jackson must have had it around 1880 – perhaps 1860 to 1880. I'm pretty sure it was he who planted the laurels and rhododendrons – as a shelter for woodcock.

It had already been broken up because when Captain Cockle bought it, he didn't buy the further wood, Tuck's Wood. He bought that later, when he also bought some of the marshes on the other side of the Fen Channel and also Crake's Marsh . He bought other bits from various people so that when we moved in, there were 180 acres of wood, carr, marsh and water.

The woods must originally have been enormous because all the adjoining fields – about 160 acres – have birch names: 'Long Birch', 'Little Birch', 'The Birch'. This indicated, and the soil indicates, too, that they were part of a birch wood.

If you take a photograph up the lane, you can see that apart from where oaks and beeches have been planted (and there has been a lot of planting in this wood), it is naturally a birch wood, with bracken underneath and some poplar.

The birch wood would have covered something like 200 acres. Obviously, some centuries ago, the main part of the birch wood was cut down for fuel, and one tends to think that – historically – this may be related to the closure of the peat pits in the 14th century, when they started to flood. Old maps show that places like Surlingham Broad were divided into narrow strips for peat digging.

So the birch would have been cut for fuel, and to heat the various small brick kilns which were scattered about the area.

Russell said that in the Napoleonic War, the birch and poplar – being very light wood – were cut and made into ammunition boxes. It was then that the wood was planted with oaks – around 1815, possibly.

In 1895, there was a very bad gale – much worse than the gales of 1976 and 1987 – and the whole of the wood was laid down except for a very few trees. Russell was born in 1900, and he distinctly remembered that the trees were still being carted away, and the whole wood came up in brambles – as indeed, it did after the 1987 gale.

His father, presumably with other people, was digging trenches and raising the soil – not so much for drainage, but to plant oaks on the raised banks in rows.

In 1976, when we had the first gale, Ted counted 150 oaks lying down, which were roughly 75-80 years old. In 1987, of course, we lost more than another 150 oaks. However, there are still some of the Napoleonic oaks standing. They are quite obvious. There are four around the 'camp fire' area and several on what I think must have been the old roadway across the carr, across the lower wood.

The lower wood has more ash and alder and sallows – and a mass of hazel. It is a wood that has been coppiced, there's no doubt, with standards – for buildings, furniture, tool handles and so on.

It was when the Cockles moved in, in 1919, that the cottages were converted into one house, and the two kitchens were made into a hallway. They had bought it in 1914, but did not come to live here until after they left Ranworth Old Hall in 1919.

The present kitchen was built about 1923, as cheaply as possible.

In 1933, Russell came to work here, doing the garden and dykes, cutting reed – which they sold. They also kept pigs and goats on Home Marsh, and chickens in the wood.

Because they kept animals, the marshes were cut – for litter. Old Mill Marsh was beautiful at that time. There were hundreds of orchids on it – I think, about five species. It was cut every year in the old-fashioned pattern. The marsh near the house, was grazed by pigs and had absolutely nothing on it except a few irises sometimes.

Russell also cut the reed – on half of Old Mill Marsh, half of Home Marsh, Crakes and Four Acres. He worked very hard.

Anyhow, during the Second World War, the tennis court (which Russell used to have to mow) fell to bits, and the grass grew up. The front, when we came here, was no longer a tennis court. You see, Russell, when the war started, had had to go and do what was considered proper agricultural work.

The wooden first floor at one end of the house was put in about 1933 – above an open loggia (now the bathroom) and a gunroom, which were already there. I don't know when the gunroom – which is now the shop – was built, but it had been Captain Cockle's study. We used it as a dining room. The door into the gunroom was through what is now the bathroom; there was no door to the gunroom through the cottage.

The Penguin, which was an Ant Wherry, had been brought up to provide extra bedrooms for the family. Captain Cockle was the only son, but he had seven sisters. His father had been a mathematician and judge in Australia. There was an enormous picture of him in the hall, in judge's robes. It touched the hall ceiling and was practically down to the floor.

I think Captain Cockle had been born in Australia.

Anyway, the seven sisters all used to come and stay, so they got this wherry – and the dyke was called 'Penguin' as a result. They made it into bedrooms. It was very nice, but two bombs fell near it during the war. Later, we did try to save it but it was too far gone. I had a picture of The Penguin, still later, with quite a large birch tree growing up through the stern.

The remains of it are still on the bank, beside Penguin Dyke.

The Covey, Surlingham 1914 'Old Scientific' Fuller (far left) and Russell's father (far right) taking marsh litter to Thorpe Station for transporting to London for cab horses

STORIES FROM FRIENDS, FAMILY AND NEIGHBOURS

Earlier this year we asked friends for any memories they had of Phyllis which they would like to share in an epilogue to her story. Thank you to everyone who has contributed.

A welcome at Wheatfen

Brian Buttery

In 1955 I obtained a Research Assistantship to work with Dr Joyce Lambert of Southampton University on the ecology of Glyceria and Phragmites around Surlingham Broad. Joyce was a native of Brundall, and knew the Ellises well. Somehow she persuaded Phyllis to take me on as a lodger during my frequent visits to Norfolk over the next three years. I am very glad that she did. Phyllis made me feel very welcome, treating me as a member of the family. In those days accommodation at Wheatfen was pretty basic: electricity was provided by a bank of large lead-acid batteries charged by a rather temperamental generator; cooking was done on the Rayburn or on Primus stoves; the toilet was primitive. The house itself consisted of two cottages that had been merged - with the result that the rooms and stairs were arranged in a somewhat eccentric manner. However, I had a comfortable bed and was very well fed. The household consisted of Phyllis and Ted, their five children and assorted visitors, like me. Russell Sewell was essentially a member of the family; he cut reed in the winter, farmed in the summer, did maintenance at any time. He was a really nice fellow. Phyllis's father John was there some of the time, as was Ted's mother Alice. Not only did Phyllis have a full-time job, cook meals and

run the household but she would find time to help load
and unload the 'tar-baby' used to transport the reed along
the river, and organise maintenance work around the
property. She always seemed to get things done.

On many evenings I could hear Phyllis on the phone dictating
Ted's daily 'column' for the Eastern Daily Press. On other
evenings there was singing around the piano. Occasionally, we
enjoyed a drop of home-brew or methaglin; sometimes a
game of scrabble; always good conversation. After a spell
in the Lab at Southampton, it was a pleasure to return to
Wheatfen and to be warmly greeted by Phyllis and the family.

Dawn McKay (nee Debenham)
In 1952 my friend Irene and I went (from Australia) to
England and taught at Mendlesham School.

The Press came and took our photo and published our
story. I told them that I had chosen this school as my
ancestors had come from Debenham and I wanted to
know more about them.

Shortly after the article appeared I had a letter from
Phyllis telling me that her ancestors were Debenhams
too. She invited us to Wheatfen to stay for a weekend.
Ted was working at the museum so we made our own
way there and he took us home. Phyllis was teaching
close by at this time.

As well as us there were other visitors: A doctor friend
and some friends of the children. I remember Russell
who seemed to be their 'Right Hand Man'.

We were made to feel completely welcome and when, in
1999 my sister Joan and I visited, again we were greeted

with the same open-hearted warmth that I remembered from so many years before.

Gill Dammers

My first memory of Phyllis, shared no doubt with hundreds of others, is of her cold unluxurious kitchen at Wheatfen, with ancient pots and pans around and windows opposite each other, one above the steel double sink. The room was usually crowded with people washing up, drying, making large numbers of cups of tea in huge pots, chatting or looking for something to eat (the younger ones naturally!). If Phyllis was there she would make sure you had a tea-towel in your hand or were doing something useful; if not you would be sent on another errand.

I remember Phyllis as being kind and determined. One did not challenge her; you did what she said. She had an excellent overview of what needed to be done and made sure it was done. In this way she provided wonderful hospitality for untold numbers of people.

When visiting Wheatfen I was impressed not only that Phyllis had taken a foster child in to her already large family but that she also looked after a friend, Russell, as though he were a brother. I still feel part of the family.

Mary Porter (nee Edwards)

I first met Phyllis in 1987 when I was on a temporary contract at the RSPB's nature reserve at Strumpshaw Fen, on the opposite side of the River Yare from Wheatfen. She was special guest to open the wildflower meadow nature trail. Straight away, typical Phyllis, we hit it off, even though we were many decades apart in age.

Soon, she asked me 'across the water' to take part in an
event to encourage more women into nature conservation.
It was a successful event, but it rained and rained. We took
shelter in her 'yellow peril' car, with me leaving from time-
to-time to feed my baby chaffinch which was perched on
the steering wheel of my car, demanding regular feeding
(and that is another story!). While sheltering she found
out that my living conditions were very basic, to put it
kindly. *"My dear, you must come over for a bath! Come any
time, whenever you need it!"*

So started a regular commute to Wheatfen. I had strict
instructions to replace the 'spider towel ladder' that was
draped over the side of the bath. It is a habit I've kept up,
years later, and it works!

It was only a year later that my mother died suddenly.
Based back in Suffolk now, I still got to Wheatfen from
time to time and have marvellous memories of newly baked
bread and Phyllis's special brew tea, a mix of Earl Grey
and something else, possibly Assam. It was delicious.
Then, my father died too. I inherited my parent's small
Border terrier, Tansy. "You must come over" said Phyllis,
gently taking me under her wing.

When I arrived, all the bedrooms were full. "Don't worry,
there's a bed in the 'kennel' (a kind of half-attic) she said.
Tansy and I tentatively bedded down for the night, perched
on floor boards. Not all the room had a floor and the
scurrying of rodents (size unknown) amongst the rafters,
very close, meant a sleepless night. At one stage, I switched
on my torch to see if Tansy was sleeping. She was sitting
bolt upright in bed, staring in the dark towards the scurrying
sounds, and shaking like a leaf. Morning couldn't come

too soon, and at six in the morning, we took shelter downstairs to have a refreshing cup of tea with our hostess. She
had already been out to check the water levels and was
full of energy.

Later that morning we went for a walk. The weather was
hot and humid. Phyllis had her shorts on, exposing thin
white legs, which were soon covered in dripping red lines
from the attentions of mosquitoes. She occasionally batted
at them, but while I was dancing about flapping at those
round me, she calmly said "*You get used to them after a while*".

A few years and two different Border Terriers later, I was
shown into the guest bedroom. With a parting instruction
of 'the net is for the hornets' gesturing towards a large
butterfly net propped up against the open window. Except
the open window brought in the dreaded mosquitoes and,
after hiding under the covers for several hours and getting
hot, I put on the light to get up to close the window, only
to find BATS flying round the room! With a groan, I switched
the light back off, confident in the powers of biological
control! I woke about six again, hearing Phyllis in the kitchen.
Opening my eyes and looking straight up at the ceiling, a
small yellow and brown face preceded by some waggling
antennae looked down at me from a small gap in the ceiling
rose of the pendant light. Before I could move, it struggled
and wiggled, and dropped out, plummeting towards me.
"Whaaaaah!" I screamed. It missed me by about a centimetre,
screeching to a halt just in time, and veered off towards
the window. I leapt out of bed, raced towards the net,
grabbed it and guided the hornet out. 'Friends and relations'
started to drop in, literally, so, getting dressed, I went
down for a cup of tea. "*You found the net then*", said Phyllis.

Once, I asked if there was anything I could do to help. *"Come out with me in the punt"* she said. *"I'm not allowed to go on my own anymore"*. So there I was queening it, lying back, being punted around a Norfolk broad by an old lady (sorry Phyllis!) and peering over the side in the water. *"Is it clear?"* asks Phyllis, worrying about the water quality. *"Can you see fish?"* I saw warblers, marsh harriers, dragon-flies... it was an idyllic afternoon.

I could go on and on; al fresco lunches, debates about nature conservation, water pollution, fundraising and events ideas. Always active and always interested in what I was doing. I still have the letters she sent me, tucked in the same box, alongside letters from Mum and Dad.

More years later, she sent me and my husband Phil £50 towards a bread-maker, as a wedding present. We still have it. I bought some Earl Grey to make a magic mix to go with it.

Thank you, Phyllis. Thank you very much indeed.

Neighbours

Tim Mack

My first memories of Phyllis Ellis are probably when I was about five and my mother used to get books from the library for her. I was about seven when she was the first person to attempt to teach me to sail. *"If you get in a muddle let go of everything"* Well, that happened on Rockland Broad with me at the helm and most of the Ellis children. Needless to say we got stuck on the mud. Unperturbed, Phyllis, who was in full skirt hopped out of the boat and pushed us off. On another occasion we were giving Phyllis a lift home from church with my grandmother in front, who remarked as we drove up to the Ellis's house "*Oh, this isn't the place, this is derelict.*" My mother's elbow was too late. But Phyllis was very amused.

More recently she has been helpful with William's projects for school, providing huge amounts of information and he has really fond memories of her.

She would do anything for anyone. Having Phyllis for a neighbour has been a real experience that we shall always treasure.

Mary Upton
Phyllis had such a strong and interesting personality. She has left a big void. My family and I shared many happy and memorable times over the years with her and Ted. Ever grateful that Phyllis played the organ for so many years.

Phyl Macdonald echoed by 'The Three Musketeers'. When Phyllis left Wheatfen the lights went out. She was always such a welcoming presence; a generous, happy person with a spontaneous laugh. She had a happy-go-lucky attitude to life and couldn't care less what other people thought. I do miss her visiting bike being thrown in to my hedge.

Hilary and Peter Bond
When we came to Surlingham, Phyllis and Ted Ellis were our next-door neighbours (half a mile away). They were a source of information and inspiration to us as they were to so many others. Over the years we came to admire Phyllis' selfless endeavours supporting all aspects of village life.

A very good friend of Phyllis was **Mike Clough**. He spent long winter evenings with her and always made sure she had plenty of firewood indoors, and took her early morning tea when she was ailing. When asked for his thoughts on Phyllis he said *"I liked the old gal. We could talk about anything."*

Barbara Rix
Phyllis was always pleased to see you and a cup of tea was a must, though I could never take to her mix of teas and would take a tea bag. She loved to talk and was interested in everything that went on in the village. In the Parish Council elections of 1994 Phyllis, at the age of 81, decided to stand again after a break of many years. Not only was she elected she came top with the most votes. The Parish Staithe was her main reason for re-joining; she was adamant that it should be under the control of the Parish Council. We spent many hours in the archives researching the history of the Staithe and found it belonged to South Norfolk District Council. After some debate they agreed to sell it to the PC. Sadly the transfer did not happen in her life-time but the eventual purchase will remain a tribute to Phyllis Ellis MBE.

Snapshots

Jake King
My abiding memory of Phyllis is that the temperature of her washing-up water was a couple of degrees below boiling and made my hands bright red and painful. Also I'll never forget the beautiful sound made by the rowlocks jangling together hanging up in the porch by the kitchen
Oh and what was that chocolate thing she made?

Lucy Paterson
The first time I met Phyllis she thrust two giant cast iron pots into my hands and said 'scrub these' I nearly fell over with the weight of them.

Hazel Crossley
Briefly:
Her face beaming benevolence from the fireside.
Her formidable backgammon playing.
Her heartfelt piano playing.
"Well, dear..." then some words of wisdom or explanation.
The freezing cold of 1969 and the bedroom window that would not shut.
The boiling hot washing up water which I tried to avoid!

Barbara Rix
She was 88, walking round the edge of the punt, her balance was amazing.

Nadia Allen
So many memories but two of my favourites:-
The first time I was there I politely offered to help with the tea (as trained by my Mum) and was told to sit down and stop making the place untidy before a huge box of chocolate concrete was placed in my lap.

In her later years, we went over for tea and she stopped chopping a dead animal and looked me sternly in the eyes and said "*I wonder what's worse, becoming a silly old fool and knowing you are, or becoming a silly old fool and not knowing*". She then continued to dismember the animal which was to be our dinner.

Andrea Burdett
She joyfully sent off Eppie the greyhound to catch the grey
squirrels around the reserve and Eppie abused her hospitality
by raiding the pantry.

Enid Thwaites
Phyllis was a powerful but kind lady who showed by example
the reward for hard work.

My son Andrew worked at Wheatfen twice, and while there,
achieved entrance to the Retained Fire Service on the
reference of Phyllis, although others had told him it would
be impossible. In fact through her encouragement Andy
achieved most of his ambitions in early life despite of severe
dyslexia and a stubborn independence. When he was 22
he had an RTA which left him severely damaged mentally
and physically. After the accident He did get to see Phyllis
again (in a wheelchair). *"You can't laze about in that for the
rest of your life – you need to get up and on with it don't you!"*
Phyllis didn't mince her words but she had a special effect
on him.

With determination he now eats and walks and is getting
back his speech. And he liked her cakes, fruit, chocolate
and jam – raspberry and rhubarb.

Once while visiting Wheatfen Phyllis came in to the office
looking tired. David asked *"Are you OK Phyllis?"* *"Yes, I've just
been doing a spot of gardening"*. This was February with snow
and ice everywhere. Now, when I go out in to the garden
my family always call it 'a spot of Phyllising' – an
unforgettable lady.

Yvonne Fuller

Visiting Wheatfen in the early 1980s my mother and I were invited in for a cup of tea before we left. Phyllis brought in a tall lidded stainless steel jug and we were told to help ourselves... we had chocolate concrete too.

John Matthews

Wheatfen was a marvellous place to take our children so I asked the three of them for their memories of Phyllis. It seems that she was just part of the package of fun; Wheatfen and Mrs Ellis – one thing. They were young, of course, but like their father had a liking for a spot of anarchy. There was a generosity that pervaded the house and that delicious, untidy garden that greatly appealed and Phyllis was undoubtedly the presiding spirit. I wouldn't have wanted to argue with her though!
I think the last time we spoke she was sitting in that tiny car – eminently practical.

Joan Tusting

I had taken down an exhibition of paintings and had them all in the boot of my car when I went to Wheatfen. Phyllis came up with the idea of exhibiting them and getting more artists involved to raise money for the Ted Ellis Trust. She approached Poppyland, a café and gallery in Horsey. Phyllis went to town. She made posters and sent the details to 'What's On' in the EDP every Thursday. When the exhibition opened the world and his wife were there. It ran all summer.

I used to pop in and see Phyllis on Fridays and have a cup of tea. She would often be out working in the garden or on the marsh. She used to say *"You used to be in the Land Army, you can help me do this!"*

Patricia Evison (née Sharman)

My family lived in Hill House, Surlingham when I was a child and I have very happy memories of Phyllis and Ted. I have lived in Southern Africa (currently Cape Town) for many years and Phyllis continued to write to me even after my parents died. This was a great pleasure to me and a loving link with my home.

Family

Suzie

While my daughter Rose was a student at Kingston University, she rang me one morning to ask if I had a copy of Mrs Beeton as her friend urgently needed a diagram of meat joints for a design project. I rang Phyllis as I knew she had one. Mum, already in her eighties, got straight on her bike, took the book up to the Post Office and, before lunchtime came round, managed (having never used the machine before) to photocopy and fax the page to Kingston successfully. This is a snapshot of a pre-internet era and gives you a flavour of P's willing spirit.

Lucy

Phyllis loved a drama.

When a torrent of rain was running down the driveway from the top field Phyllis called for us all to grab spades and dig a channel across the road to divert the water in to the dyke, so preventing the garage from flooding, meanwhile soaking us all to the skin!

She was persuasive and found endless ways to keep us occupied. She liked to give us jobs that were fun, useful and healthy:

– Wrapping rags round our feet to enable fast, smooth
sliding up and down the hall floor to polish it.
– Providing us with knives to dig out the earth between
the squares along the backyard path.
– Hooking glyceria hovers to the back of the boat in
order to drag them out to the Broad.
– Collecting rain water from dripping gutters in bowls
and tins then using it to wash our hair. This was
especially exciting as we were allowed to play in the rain
and the sounds were musical.

She encouraged us to keep busy whatever and I shall
always be grateful to her for that.

She will always be remembered for her endless generosity.
She loved to have lots of people around and to keep them
busy. She was unremittingly enduring – juggling the provision
of food, the sorting out of mattresses for visitors, managing
without electricity and running water and keeping going,
despite a full time teaching job and cycling to school and
back in all weathers. Tough, determined, robust and
resilient, she rarely took a day off for illness.

Mum enjoyed getting dressed up for a night out but it
was never a priority. She put herself last.

Mary
I came home from work one day and was surprised to
find Phyllis, in her eighties, at the top of a very tall ladder
painting the outside of our house. *"Well, dear, I am old and
I'd rather die falling off a ladder doing something useful than
linger in hospital"*

Mum loved dancing and we often used to dance around

while some members of the family played their musical instruments. Towards the end of her life she was a little less steady on her feet and on the eve of her final abseil her enthusiastic waltzing ended with us on the floor with a heavy wrought iron lamp stand on top of us. She made no fuss but after the abseil we found she had strapped up her torso, assuming she had a broken rib. She did not complain about illness or infirmity.

The last time we danced was on her 90th birthday on the lawn. *"I WILL dance"* she said. And she did.

Phyllis in her 'puttees'

CHOCOLATE CONCRETE

Phyllis made her own version of a recipe for chocolate squares which her daughter Mary gave her in 1981. Until then her standbys had been fruit cake, shortbread and flapjack. It is a very simple recipe to which Phyllis added glace cherries and sometimes stem ginger. The label 'concrete' was added by the family after one particular 'tooth-breaking' version which had been left in the oven too long. In her later years she sometimes gave a slightly confusing recipe to various people so this is to put the record straight!

Recipe

Mix together:
1 cup each SR flour, desiccated coconut or chopped nuts,
Crushed weetabix (about 3),
¼ cup sugar, 1 tbsp cocoa powder.

Melt 4 oz butter or marge and 1 tbsp golden syrup.
Stir into the dry mixture.

Press down in greased Swiss roll tin.

Bake at 350C/177F 10 mins for soft, 15-20 mins for harder.

Cover with squares of plain chocolate and put back in oven for a short while for chocolate to melt. Spread melted chocolate evenly. Cut into squares when cooled.

Actually any flour, nuts, cereal, sugar, marge or butter work OK. The cherries or ginger add class!

ABOUT THE TED ELLIS TRUST
AND THE FUTURE OF WHEATFEN BROAD

Phyllis was married for 48 years to the well-known writer
and broadcaster Ted Ellis (Edward Augustine Ellis DSc FLS
1909-1986) and together they spent a lifetime devoted to
natural history and education.

Ted was born in Guernsey of Norfolk parents who returned
to Great Yarmouth in 1920. He was Keeper of Natural
History at the Castle Museum, Norwich from 1928-1956.
For forty years he lived with his family at Wheatfen Broad,
Surlingham in a remote cottage amongst 130 acres of
woodland and fen and became well-known as one of the
great characters of East Anglia. Although he was a serious
naturalist with a national reputation, whose research work
was meticulous and highly respected by the academic world,
he was a man who had the ability to communicate his
enthusiasm to everyone.

Such a rich contribution deserves to be remembered and
after Ted died, Phyllis founded the Ted Ellis Trust to do just
that – by preserving Wheatfen Broad as a nature reserve.

Wheatfen is a strange primitive area recognised as a Site
of Special Scientific Interest and is one of the last tidal
marshes of the Yare Valley. The Trust wants to preserve
its rich and fragile ecology, but above all, it wants to keep
this land and its wildlife accessible for the enjoyment and
education of children, students and everyone interested
in Nature. That is what Ted would have wanted too.

Wheatfen Broad is a remainder of the once extensive Yare Valley swamp. It is, undoubtedly, one of the most important sites of its kind in Britain.

As the patron of the Trust, David Bellamy said, "*Wheatfen Broad is, in its way, as important as Mount Everest or the giant redwood forests of North America. It is probably the best bit of fenland we have because we know so much about it. That is purely because one man gave his life trying to understand it - Ted Ellis*".

Wheatfen is now managed as a nature reserve and consists largely of open fen, reed beds, sallow carr and the small broads Wheatfen and Deep Waters.

The house and adjacent land are still owned and occupied by the family who allow The Trust to extend the nature trails into Surlingham Wood and The Carr.

There is no charge for entry but contributions towards the upkeep of the reserve are always very welcome.

If you would like to support this work by joining the Friends of the Ted Ellis Trust, you can do so on the Ted Ellis Trust website: www.wheatfen.org

As a member of the Friends you will receive an annual newsletter featuring news from Wheatfen and natural history-related articles.

You can view pictures taken at Wheatfen, recent and historic, at www.flickr.com/groups/wheatfen.

Facebook subscribers can also keep up to date with news and events by joining the group Wheatfen – The Ted Ellis Trust Nature Reserve

Phyllis with daughters Lucy, Suzie and Mary